WATT
1464
4TWA

W9-COL-269

119

WATERLOO HIGH SCHOOL LIBRARY
1464 INDUSTRY RD.
ATWATER OHIO 44201

AIDS

Other Books of Related Interest in the Opposing Viewpoints Series:

Biomedical Ethics
Chemical Dependency
Death & Dying
Sexual Values
Teenage Sexuality

Additional Books in the Opposing Viewpoints Series:

Abortion
American Foreign Policy
American Government
The American Military
American Values
America's Prisons
The Arms Race
Censorship
Central America
Constructing a Life Philosophy
Crime & Criminals
Criminal Justice
The Death Penalty
Drug Abuse
Economics in America
The Environmental Crisis
Latin America
Male/Female Roles
The Mass Media
The Middle East
Nuclear War
The Political Spectrum
Problems of Africa
Science and Religion
Social Justice
The Soviet Union
Terrorism
The Vietnam War
War and Human Nature
The Welfare State

WATERLOO HIGH SCHOOL LIBRARY
1464 INDUSTRY RD.
ATWATER, OHIO 44201

AIDS

David L. Bender & Bruno Leone, *Series Editors*

Lynn Hall & Thomas Modl, *Book Editors*

OPPOSING VIEWPOINTS SERIES ®

Greenhaven Press   577 Shoreview Park Road   St. Paul, Minnesota 55126

362.1
Aid

No part of this book may be reproduced or used in any other form or by any other means, electrical, mechanical or otherwise, including, but not limited to photocopy, recording or any information storage and retrieval system, without prior written permission from the publisher.

Library of Congress Cataloging-in-Publication Data

AIDS : opposing viewpoints.

(Opposing viewpoints series)
Bibliography: p.
Includes index.
1. AIDS (Disease)—Popular works. 2. AIDS
(Disease)—Social aspects. I. Hall, Lynn, 1949-
II. Modl, Thomas, 1963-   . III. Series.
[DNLM: 1. Acquired Immunodeficiency Syndrome—popular
works. WD 308 A28764]
RC607.A26A3485   1988   362.1'9697'92   87-14834
ISBN 0-89908-427-3
ISBN 0-89908-402-8 (pbk.)

© Copyright 1988 by Greenhaven Press, Inc.

WATERLOO HIGH SCHOOL LIBRARY
1464 INDUSTRY RD.
ATWATER, OHIO 44201

"Congress shall make no law . . . abridging the freedom of speech, or of the press."

First Amendment to the US Constitution

The basic foundation of our democracy is the first amendment guarantee of freedom of expression. The *Opposing Viewpoints Series* is dedicated to the concept of this basic freedom and the idea that it is more important to practice it than to enshrine it.

Contents

Chapter 3: Will Controlling AIDS Undermine Civil Rights?

Chapter 4: Is the Government's Response to AIDS Adequate?

Why Consider Opposing Viewpoints?

"It is better to debate a question without settling it than to settle a question without debating it."

Joseph Joubert (1754-1824)

The Importance of Examining Opposing Viewpoints

The purpose of the Opposing Viewpoints books, and this book in particular, is to present balanced, and often difficult to find, opposing points of view on complex and sensitive issues.

Probably the best way to become informed is to analyze the positions of those who are regarded as experts and well studied on issues. It is important to consider every variety of opinion in an attempt to determine the truth. Opinions from the mainstream of society should be examined. But also important are opinions that are considered radical, reactionary, or minority as well as those stigmatized by some other uncomplimentary label. An important lesson of history is the eventual acceptance of many unpopular and even despised opinions. The ideas of Socrates, Jesus, and Galileo are good examples of this.

Readers will approach this book with their own opinions on the issues debated within it. However, to have a good grasp of one's own viewpoint, it is necessary to understand the arguments of those with whom one disagrees. It can be said that those who do not completely understand their adversary's point of view do not fully understand their own.

A persuasive case for considering opposing viewpoints has been presented by John Stuart Mill in his work *On Liberty*. When examining controversial issues it may be helpful to reflect on this suggestion:

> The only way in which a human being can make some approach to knowing the whole of a subject, is by hearing what can be said about it by persons of every variety of opinion, and studying all modes in which it can be looked at by every character of mind. No wise man ever acquired his wisdom in any mode but this.

Analyzing Sources of Information

The Opposing Viewpoints books include diverse materials taken from magazines, journals, books, and newspapers, as well as statements and position papers from a wide range of individuals, organizations and governments. This broad spectrum of sources helps to develop patterns of thinking which are open to the consideration of a variety of opinions.

Pitfalls To Avoid

A pitfall to avoid in considering opposing points of view is that of regarding one's own opinion as being common sense and the most rational stance and the point of view of others as being only opinion and naturally wrong. It may be that another's opinion is correct and one's own is in error.

Another pitfall to avoid is that of closing one's mind to the opinions of those with whom one disagrees. The best way to approach a dialogue is to make one's primary purpose that of understanding the mind and arguments of the other person and not that of enlightening him or her with one's own solutions. More can be learned by listening than speaking.

It is my hope that after reading this book the reader will have a deeper understanding of the issues debated and will appreciate the complexity of even seemingly simple issues on which good and honest people disagree. This awareness is particularly important in a democratic society such as ours where people enter into public debate to determine the common good. Those with whom one disagrees should not necessarily be regarded as enemies, but perhaps simply as people who suggest different paths to a common goal.

Developing Basic Reading and Thinking Skills

In this book carefully edited opposing viewpoints are purposely placed back to back to create a running debate; each viewpoint is preceded by a short quotation that best expresses the author's main argument. This format instantly plunges the reader into the midst of a controversial issue and greatly aids that reader in mastering the basic skill of recognizing an author's point of view.

A number of basic skills for critical thinking are practiced in the activities that appear throughout the books in the series. Some of the skills are:

Evaluating Sources of Information The ability to choose from among alternative sources the most reliable and accurate source in relation to a given subject.

Separating Fact from Opinion The ability to make the basic distinction between factual statements (those that can be demonstrated or verified empirically) and statements of opinion (those that are beliefs or attitudes that cannot be proved).

Identifying Stereotypes The ability to identify oversimplified, exaggerated descriptions (favorable or unfavorable) about people and insulting statements about racial, religious or national groups, based upon misinformation or lack of information.

Recognizing Ethnocentrism The ability to recognize attitudes or opinions that express the view that one's own race, culture, or group is inherently superior, or those attitudes that judge another culture or group in terms of one's own.

It is important to consider opposing viewpoints and equally important to be able to critically analyze those viewpoints. The activities in this book are designed to help the reader master these thinking skills. Statements are taken from the book's viewpoints and the reader is asked to analyze them. This technique aids the reader in developing skills that not only can be applied to the viewpoints in this book, but also to situations where opinionated spokespersons comment on controversial issues. Although the activities are helpful to the solitary reader, they are most useful when the reader can benefit from the interaction of group discussion.

Using this book and others in the series should help readers develop basic reading and thinking skills. These skills should improve the readers' ability to understand what they read. Readers should be better able to separate fact from opinion, substance from rhetoric and become better consumers of information in our media-centered culture.

This volume of the Opposing Viewpoints books does not advocate a particular point of view. Quite the contrary! The very nature of the book leaves it to the reader to formulate the opinions he or she finds most suitable. My purpose as publisher is to see that this is made possible by offering a wide range of viewpoints which are fairly presented.

David L. Bender
Publisher

Introduction

"Not since syphilis among the Spanish, plague among the French, tuberculosis among the Eskimos, and smallpox among the American Indians has there been the threat of such a scourge."

Journal of the American Medical Association, *1985*

AIDS can easily be deemed the world's most serious health issue since the bubonic plague of the 14th century. Indeed, many social commentators have called AIDS the "new plague." Every person who develops the AIDS disease dies. In Africa, whole villages have fallen victim to the disease. While these African villages seem remote to the US and other nations, there is a rapidly rising fear of a pandemic outbreak of AIDS. When the disease was first identified in 1977, the public showed few signs of concern since AIDS seemed relegated to the homosexual and drug-using communities. This indifference vanished when the disease began attacking the heterosexual population as well.

As scientists continue to search for a cure for AIDS, the question of whether AIDS is merely a new disease or a timeless problem remains: In spite of our vast technological knowledge of the body and disease, humanity is still susceptible to new, virulent, viruses. A vast chasm of scientific understanding separates the 1980s from the 1300s yet the victims of AIDS are not very different from those victims of past "mysterious" diseases like the bubonic plague or polio. It remains to be seen whether or not AIDS is more like polio, for which modern medicine found a quick, effective preventative, or more like the bubonic plague, from which countless numbers of people in Europe and Asia died.

In 1986, the Surgeon General of the US, C. Everett Koop, issued a report on the AIDS virus. The report contains a clear, concise description of the virus and its spread. The editors have excerpted the following sections from the report as an overview of the disease.

C. Everett Koop, *Surgeon General's Report on Acquired Immune Deficiency Syndrome*, U.S. Department of Health and Human Services, 1986.

The Surgeon General's Report

The letters A-I-D-S stand for Acquired Immune Deficiency Syndrome. When a person is sick with AIDS, he/she is in the final stages of a series of health problems caused by a virus (germ) that can be passed from one person to another chiefly during sexual contact or through the sharing of intravenous drug needles and syringes used for "shooting" drugs. Scientists have named the AIDS virus "HIV or HTLV-III or LAV." These abbreviations stand for information denoting a virus that attacks white blood cells (T-Lymphocytes) in the human blood. The AIDS virus attacks a person's immune system and damages his/her ability to fight other disease. Without a functioning immune system to ward off other germs, he/she now becomes vulnerable to becoming infected by bacteria, protozoa, fungi, and other viruses and malignancies, which may cause life-threatening illness, such as pneumonia, meningitis, and cancer.

There is presently no cure for AIDS. There is presently no vaccine to prevent AIDS.

When the AIDS virus enters the blood stream, it begins to attack certain white blood cells (T-Lymphocytes). Substances called antibodies are produced by the body. These antibodies can be detected in the blood by a simple test, usually two weeks to three months after infection. Even before the antibody test is positive, the victim can pass the virus to others.

Once an individual is infected, there are several possibilities. Some people may remain well but even so they are able to infect others. . . . In some people the protective immune system may be destroyed by the virus and then other germs (bacteria, protozoa, fungi and other viruses) and cancers that ordinarily would never get a foothold cause "opportunistic diseases"—using the *opportunity* of lowered resistance to infect and destroy. Some of the most common are *Pneumocystis carinii* pneumonia and tuberculosis. Individuals infected with the AIDS virus may also develop certain types of cancers such as Kaposi's sarcoma. These infected people have classic AIDS. Evidence shows that the AIDS virus may also attack the nervous system, causing damage to the brain.

Signs and Symptoms

Some people remain apparently well after infection with the AIDS virus. They may have no physically apparent symptoms of illness. However, if proper precautions are not used with sexual contacts and/or intravenous drug use, these infected individuals can spread the virus to others. Anyone

14

who thinks he or she is infected or involved in high risk behaviors should not donate his/her blood, organs, tissues, or sperm because they may now contain the AIDS virus. . . .

Only a qualified health professional can diagnose AIDS, which is the result of a natural progress of infection by the AIDS virus. AIDS destroys the body's immune (defense) system and allows otherwise controllable infections to invade the body and cause additional diseases. These opportunistic diseases would not otherwise gain a foothold in the body. These opportunistic diseases may eventually cause death.

Some symptoms and signs of AIDS and the "opportunistic infections" may include a persistent cough and fever associated with shortness of breath or difficult breathing and may be the symptoms of *Pneumocystis carinii* pneumonia. Multiple purplish blotches and bumps on the skin may be a sign of Kaposi's sarcoma. The AIDS virus in all infected people is essentially the same; the reactions of individuals may differ.

The AIDS virus may also attack the nervous system and cause delayed damage to the brain. This damage may take years to develop and the symptoms may show up as memory loss, indifference, loss of coordination, partial paralysis, or mental disorder. These symptoms may occur alone, or with other symptoms mentioned earlier.

The Present Situation

People infected with the AIDS virus . . . are assumed to be capable of spreading the virus sexually (heterosexually or homosexually) or by sharing needles and syringes or other implements for intravenous drug use. . . . It is difficult to predict the number who will develop AIDS because symptoms sometimes take as long as nine years to show up. With our present knowledge, scientists predict that 20 to 30 percent of those infected with the AIDS virus will develop an illness that fits an accepted definition of AIDS within five years. . . .

The majority of infected antibody positive individuals who carry the AIDS virus show no disease symptoms and may not come down with the disease for many years, if ever. . . .

Although AIDS is still a mysterious disease in many ways, our scientists have learned a great deal about it. In five years we know more about AIDS than many diseases that we have studied for even longer periods. While there is no vaccine or cure, the results from the health and behavioral research community can only add to our knowledge and increase our understanding of the disease and ways to prevent and treat it.

In spite of all that is known about transmission of the AIDS virus, scientists will learn more. One possibility is the potential discovery of factors that may better explain the mechanism of AIDS infection.

Why are the antibodies produced by the body to fight the AIDS virus not able to destroy that virus?

The antibodies detected in the blood of carriers of the AIDS virus are ineffective, at least when classic AIDS is actually triggered. They cannot check the damage caused by the virus, which is by then present in large numbers in the body. Researchers cannot explain this important observation. We still do not know why the AIDS virus is not destroyed by man's immune system.

The Focus of This Book

The editors of *AIDS: Opposing Viewpoints* have collected a wide variety of opinions on five key issues. The topics debated are: How Serious Is AIDS? How Can AIDS Be Controlled? Will Controlling AIDS Undermine Civil Rights? Is the Government's Response to AIDS Adequate? and How Will AIDS Affect Society? Many aspects of the AIDS problem continue to be debated, and many medical facts and assumptions about this disease may change. For this reason, every effort has been made to focus on debates that will continue to be concerns until that hopeful day when an effective vaccine and/or cure for AIDS is discovered.

How Serious Is AIDS?

Chapter Preface

In 1977, medical journals carried articles reporting on a pneumonia-like illness that affected mostly homosexual males and intravenous drug users. The disease came to be known as AIDS. The virus gained national attention in 1981, largely due to evidence that it could be spread to the heterosexual population. This knowledge alarmed physicians and and the general public. But whether or not the alarm is warranted remains arguable. Is AIDS a modern-day plague? Or is it confined to a few high-risk groups? Should panic, calm, or indifference be society's response?

The authors in this chapter debate just how vulnerable society is to the AIDS virus. Their arguments show that there remains considerable disagreement about the important and dangerous nature of AIDS.

"Daily the problem grows even more enormous, and very soon hundreds of thousands of Americans will be stricken [with AIDS.]"

AIDS Is a Serious Problem for All

Neil R. Schram

Neil R. Schram is an internist and a director of the Los Angeles City/County AIDS Task Force. The following viewpoint consists of two separate articles that he wrote which appeared in the *Los Angeles Times*. In Part I, Schram states that projections of the increasing spread of AIDS made by the US Public Health Service are not being taken seriously. The enormity of the problem must be communicated to everyone. In Part II, Schram claims that society has refused to face the realities of the AIDS crisis and concludes with a list of actions that he believes would effectively slow down AIDS.

As you read, consider the following questions:

1. Why does Schram believe there has not been adequate funding for AIDS programs?
2. Why, according to Schram, are public health officials reluctant to clearly state the seriousness of the risk of AIDS infection to heterosexuals?
3. In the opinion of the author, how is denial of the seriousness of the AIDS epidemic contributing to the continuance of hazardous health habits?

Neil R. Schram, "When Will We Take AIDS Seriously?" *Los Angeles Times*, June 20, 1986.
Neil R. Schram, "1987 Could Be the Year Showing a Slowdown in AIDS Spread—If. . ." *Los Angeles Times*, December 31, 1986. Reprinted with the author's permission.

I

The AIDS epidemic has been with us [since 1981]. The staggering projections made recently by the U.S. Public Health Service show that the epidemic will be with us for at least another five years.

The PHS predicts that a cumulative 270,000 cases of AIDS will be reported by the end of 1991 (compared with 21,000 by June, 1986); 3,000 will involve infants and children, most of them infected before birth. During 1991 alone, 145,000 people with AIDS will be requiring medical care. The PHS estimates that there also will be an additional 55,000 cases of misdiagnosed or unreported AIDS. The agency is unable to estimate how many people will be infected but showing no symptoms over the next five years. It does, however, forecast an exponential growth of AIDS due to heterosexual contact from 1,100 cases this year to 7,000 in 1991. . . .

Society's Disturbing Lack of Will

What is most disturbing is that we have the knowledge to prevent most of those infections, but, as a society, we do not have the will. We have allowed a vocal, highly political minority to misappropriate AIDS as a moral issue, giving our government leaders an excuse to abdicate their responsibility for the health and welfare of us all.

AIDS is a health issue, and as a physician I am especially disturbed to see how reluctant my colleagues are to assume their role in the first line of defense against the epidemic. Unfortunately, physicians are most comfortable discussing viruses and symptoms of disease. Discussing sex is very difficult (as it is for patients). As a result, few physicians include questions about sexual activity as part of a routine health examination. Fewer still are likely to ask if a patient is at risk specifically for AIDS, and provide appropriate advice.

Serious Need for Funding

The group at highest risk is gay and bisexual men. With substantial numbers of AIDS cases now reported in all major cities, the gay community should be mounting large-scale prevention programs around the country similar to the program in San Francisco. This effort requires large funding. However, the money is not forthcoming, because too many politicians fear that advocating such funding would be interpreted as condoning or encouraging homosexuality.

Adding to the gay community's problem is the activism of some people who want to reverse the civil-rights advances that lesbians and gay men have made over the last 20 years and are using AIDS to attack those civil rights. Thus the resources that the gay community could apply to fighting the spread of the virus are diverted to battling politicians and homophobes.

Intravenous drug users constitute the second group at risk, primarily from sharing needles or equipment. It is obvious that providing sterile needles, as is done in the Netherlands, would be a significant preventive response. But, again, that is not acceptable politically. Nor is a major financial commitment to counselors and expansion of methadone maintenance programs. This is with the full knowledge that IV drug users are heterosexually active and will spread the virus to their sexual contacts (who can spread it to theirs) and their unborn children.

It is known that for a women infected with the AIDS virus,

A ONE-MAN AIDS EPIDEMIC

AIDS

AIDS-related complex (ARC)

Not infected

PARTNERS IN BELGIUM

PARTNERS IN AFRICA

BELGIUM

AFRICA

Note: All data are preliminary evidence; more people were probably infected.

USN&WR— Basic data: Dr. Nathan Clumeck of St. Pierre Hospital in Brussels, Belgium

A still unraveling case shows starkly how one person, though heterosexual, can scatter the AIDS virus. A black Belgian businessman is being investigated by Dr. Nathan Clumeck, a specialist in infectious diseases. The man, by all accounts exclusively heterosexual, made regular business trips to Africa. He had at least 12 sexual partners there and in Belgium, all but one of them white, middle-class women who had met him at parties. None was promiscuous, none used drugs, and all had only vaginal intercourse with the man. The source of his AIDS is unknown. Nine of the 12 women have developed AIDS or AIDS-related complex (ARC), a precursor to the disease. One of the known sex partners of these women has ARC, and three more of their partners have tested negative. Three of the 12 women have tested negative. The man, diagnosed as having AIDS in November of 1985, died at 40 last February.

Copyright, 1987, U.S. News & World Report. Reprinted from issue of Jan. 12, 1987.

pregnancy increases her chances of developing AIDS. The risk that the child will also be infected with the virus is substantial. The Public Health Service currently advises that parents who are at risk for AIDS be tested before pregnancy and refrain from pregnancy if either parent tests positive. That advice is clearly inadequate. Where either parent is at risk, both parents should be tested. If either parent is confirmed positive, abortion should be strongly advised. Again, this advice is politically unacceptable. Thus we expect 3,000 AIDS cases in children by 1991, and countless other infected children who won't develop the disease but are likely to be carriers for life.

It is estimated that there are 50 to 100 people infected for every person diagnosed as having AIDS. Thus by 1991 there may well be 500,000 to 1 million heterosexuals infected with the AIDS virus. Yet many heterosexuals cling to the ridiculous notion that this is a "gay disease." Contributing to this societywide denial is the reluctance of public health officials to state the risk clearly for fear of causing panic. However, the figures are there for all to see. In the same week that the PHS projections were made, the weekly AIDS report by the Centers for Disease Control showed that the number of cases due to heterosexual spread have risen for the first time from 1% of the total to 2%. And a significant part of the 6% of AIDS cases listed as "unknown cause" are thought likely to be due to heterosexual spread.

What Society Must Do

For years we have recognized what is needed to slow this epidemic: an appreciation of the enormity of the problem so that we can mobilize our available resources. Daily the problem grows even more enormous, and very soon hundreds of thousands of Americans will be stricken. Apart from the unspeakable suffering of these victims and their loved ones, the tragedy is that our society is so immobilized by prudishness or politics or moralizing that we cannot or will not deal with these issues.

II

Denial is a wonderful survival device. It allows us to drive a car every day without believing that we will be among the tens of thousands of people who die each year in car accidents. Denial also is an insidious device of self-destruction. It allows people to continue with habits hazardous to their health in the belief that they will remain on the right side of the odds. In the past few years, denial has been working overtime against efforts to educate people about the AIDS epidemic.

Most Americans are heterosexual; most Americans do not use injectable drugs. AIDS is a "gay disease," most Americans say. Or "people who shoot up are only killing themselves; what's it to me?"

This is what it means to us all:

Between 1 million and 1½ million Americans are now carrying the AIDS virus; even if the spread of the virus stopped today, it is believed that 250,000 to 750,000 would come down with the full-blown disease within 10 years.

Of course, the virus will not be stopped in the foreseeable future. In fact, what makes this epidemic so frightening is the researchers' belief that the AIDS virus stays in the body—and keeps that person potentially infectious—for life. This characteristic makes AIDS unique in deadliness. In the two epidemics that Americans remember vividly, influenza and polio, those stricken were infectious for only a short time.

AIDS Victims Are "Us"

So long as AIDS could be thought of as "the gay disease," as the ultimate wage of sinners, we could think ourselves better.

But now AIDS attacks those we love. We confront our humanity. . . .

In Africa, AIDS seems to be spread mostly through heterosexual intercourse.

That fact must frighten us all.

AIDS means death.

AIDS is proving that it kills regardless of sex, race, age, politics, or religion. It kills just as dispassionately as did polio, tuberculosis, smallpox, or plague. . . .

And we all seem scared.

An astonishing 54 percent of us want to see victims of AIDS quarantined, says Gallup. Such fears have fueled political tyrants in years past. But the victims are no longer "the homosexuals" or "the drug abusers."

"They" are us.

And our best defense is our shared humanity.

Lawrence Wade, *The Washington Times*, November 19, 1986.

Even more pertinent to the "so what" crowd, at present most AIDS carriers are unaware that they are infected. So every unprotected sexual encounter outside a longstanding monogamous relationship is a major gamble.

An AIDS Scenario

In 1986 every key health authority in the United States addressed the AIDS crisis, culminating with Surgeon General C. Everett Koop's extraordinary and welcome statement, which made excellent recommendations about AIDS. Still, regrettably, 1986 will

WATERLOO HIGH SCHOOL LIBRARY
1464 INDUSTRY RD.
ATWATER, OHIO 44201

not be remembered as the year when society as a whole took the crisis seriously enough to confront it realistically and effectively. What if we managed to make [this year] different? This is what would happen:

We would stop dividing people with AIDS into "innocent victims" (children and blood-product recipients) and, therefore by implication, "guilty-ones" (gay and bisexual men, intravenous drug users and "promiscuous" heterosexuals).

We would accept that homosexuality is as much a part of one's makeup as left-handedness and stop attributing this tragic epidemic to God's wrath. (Why are lesbians virtually AIDS-free if AIDS were divine retribution for homosexuality?)

The gay community would recognize that the AIDS virus represents a greater threat to its survival than civil-rights attacks do. A community commitment by gay men and lesbians to help prevent the spread of the virus would foster individual and collective responsibility, which would then be helpful in resisting civil-rights attacks as well.

Prevent the Spread of AIDS

We would spend money to help intravenous drug users quit their habits, not only because we want to prevent the spread of AIDS to their sexual partners and unborn children but also because we want to prevent them, as people, from getting this terrible disease.

Physicians would overcome their difficulties in dealing with sexual matters and would learn how to determine which of their patients are at risk from AIDS and how to counsel them on minimizing that risk.

The media would recognize that the epidemic of AIDS does not fit into their customary handling of sex-related news. So they would provide regular, detailed, educational information about how the virus is and is not spread. And they would accept advertising and public-service announcements for condoms, which can help prevent not only unwanted pregnancies but the spread of the AIDS virus as well.

Parents would insist that schools begin the AIDS education programs recommended by the surgeon general.

Admit the Seriousness of the Epidemic

President Reagan would acknowledge the seriousness of the epidemic and publicly support the recommendations of the surgeon general. The President would also advocate funding to accomplish those recommendations.

Politicians would overcome their reluctance to take the lead in AIDS funding for education and prevention, and would spend the money on those areas as well as for research and patient needs.

The Justice Department . . . would recognize the reality and inappropriateness of employment discrimination against people hav-

24

ing AIDS, and would work to oppose such discrimination.

Pre-paid health plans would recognize that this epidemic will severely affect them all. They would stop trying to "select out" potential AIDS clients, and would turn their efforts to preventive education and saving lives.

Hospitals and medical centers would have mandatory education programs for personnel to allay their fears about the disease and to improve medical care for people with AIDS.

Employers would initiate workplace programs concerning AIDS, whether or not they have employees diagnosed with the disease.

Black and Latino community leadership, including the church, would recognize that minorities are being affected out of proportion to their numbers in this country and would join the battle against AIDS.

AIDS Is Unique

Society would recognize that AIDS is unique, and would stop trying to make the disease fit established patterns and rules, since the virus will not behave as we want it to.

Americans would stop being able to have sex while being unable to talk about it. Explicit talk about sex would occur in the media, in the workplace, in the home and, most important, between two people about to have sex.

It Would Only Be a Start

All people would show compassion and sensitivity to people with AIDS and stop blaming them for their disease.

If all this came to pass, [this] would be known as the year the spread of the AIDS virus began to slow in the United States. Even then it would only be a start in the very long siege ahead of us.

"With so many experts dramatizing the epidemic, it's little wonder that those who depend on their advice are coming to believe that AIDS is already as rampant as influenza."

AIDS Is Not a Serious Problem for All

Suzanne Fields and *The New York Times*

Suzanne Fields is a columnist for *The Washington Times*. In Part I of the following viewpoint, she argues that there is a campaign to frighten heterosexuals into identifying with the high risk AIDS groups by misrepresenting transmission statistics. *The New York Times* has frequently stated that society's extreme fear of AIDS is just that, fear. In Part II of the following viewpoint, a *Times* editorial contends that while there are legitimate reasons for concern about AIDS, exaggeration creates false fears.

As you read, consider the following questions:

1. What evidence does Fields cite to prove that old statistics have been skewed to show an increase of AIDS among heterosexuals?
2. Why do the *Times* editors believe that for the foreseeable future AIDS will stay confined to the known high risk groups?
3. What, in the opinion of the *Times* editors, might be gained by special interest groups in exaggerating the fears of heterosexual transmission?

Suzanne Fields, "Misrepresenting AIDS," *The Washington Times*, August 7, 1986. Reprinted with permission.
The New York Times, "AIDS Alarms, and False Alarms," February 4, 1987. Copyright © 1987 by The New York Times Company. Reprinted by permission.

Has AIDS become a disease for all of us?

The campaign to make heterosexuals think so continues—a campaign to frighten them into a closer identification with homosexuals and intravenous drug users, the high-risk groups for AIDS. It seems to be based on the presumption that such identification will heighten compassion, increase the federal money available to researchers, and speed a cure.

It's a strange strategy of irrationality, pushed by the very people who should be applying reason to a cruel and heart-breaking enigma.

Misreading the Facts

Columnist Ellen Goodman, for example, thinks of AIDS as an Equal Opportunity Infector. "What does it take," she asks, "to realize that a deadly virus doesn't discriminate on the basis of race, sex, or sexual orientation?"

Such a formulation might be an amusing twisting of semantics, except that it sadly misreads the facts. She arrives at her notion when she receives a sorrowful letter from a mother who discovers that her "dean's list" daughter has tested positive for the AIDS virus. (As terrific as making the dean's list is, it carries with it no immunity to any known disease, so far as anyone now knows.)

"I admit that I skimmed this letter looking for clues," Miss Goodman writes. "Was her daughter a drug user? Did she have a bisexual lover? Had she received blood? But there were no hints and so I was unable to separate my own family from hers into a safety zone."

I don't know what kind of hints would have satisfied Miss Goodman, but surely a mother of a college student is among the last ones on Earth to be conversant with the evidence of the risks and dangers of a daughter's secret life. Short of knowing details about her daughter's male friends, the nature of her sexual acts, whether, on the whim of a single moment, she ever pushed a polluted needle into her body, a mother knows very little. . . .

Rearranged Statistics

The facts about AIDS are sad enough without varnishing them with misrepresentation. A national tragedy of broken young lives needs no embellishment; we need no participation of heterosexuals to make us grieve for homosexual victims.

What we have is not new evidence, but rearranged statistics.

Until [August 1986]. . . , the federal Centers for Disease Control reported that heterosexuals made up a fairly constant 2 percent of the diagnosed cases of AIDS. The statisticians now say that AIDS has risen to 4 percent among heterosexuals. The rise owes more to an "altered category" than to altered percentages.

Of the 862 heterosexuals who have been diagnosed as having AIDS, 483—or more than half—were born in Haiti or in central and east Africa. Haitians once were classified as a separate high-risk group for AIDS, but researchers decided that it unfairly stigmatized them. Haitians were moved into the heterosexual category. The decision was political, not medical.

There's "strong evidence," says Dr. Harold Jaffe, chief of the epidemiology branch of CDC, that AIDS is transmitted among Haitians heterosexually.

Statistics Need Better Understanding

That may be, but an understanding of the statistics is important. Certain studies indicate that one person in 20 has been exposed to AIDS in Haiti, compared to one in 10,000 in the United States. That is a big difference for people occupying the same category.

No Reason for Hysteria

There's no doubt that the pool of infection is widening, and that AIDS may be "going somewhere," as one government researcher puts it. But how fast, and how far, is open to conjecture, and while there's reason for concern—as there is over any lethal disease—there's none for hysteria. Given what's known about the way the AIDS virus is transmitted, it's highly unlikely that it will become a threat to society as a whole, at least not in Europe or the U.S. . . .

What can be said with a good deal of certainty is that AIDS in the U.S. will remain overwhelmingly confined, in the foreseeable future, to the current risk populations—homosexuals, IV drug abusers, and, to a much smaller extent, blood recipients—and that the hard-to-spread virus isn't likely to become any more contagious. If AIDS is going to spread heterosexually, it will do so primarily through the enormous pool of heroin addicts, male and female, and not through conventional sexual contacts between "straight" men and women.

John Langone, *Discover*, September 1986.

Only 379 heterosexuals born in this country have AIDS, less than 2 percent of the 22,792 diagnosed cases. Dr. Jaffe says he does not expect a pattern of heterosexual transmissions such as those observed in Haiti and central Africa to occur in the United States. He can speak with some confidence: the 2 percent figure—it's 1.6 percent, to be more precise—has varied almost imperceptibly over the months.

"The majority of cases will continue to be homosexual men, drug abusers, and, to a lesser degree, transfusion cases," he told *The New York Times*. Dr. Jaffe says the chances of infection for a heterosexual not having sex with any risk-group members are extremely low.

Misleading numbers of heterosexual cases have also been derived from the Army, which reported one study in which 15 out of 41 cases of AIDS were said to come through heterosexual contact. You don't have to be an expert to question these statistics, though many experts do, too. Would a homosexual or a drug addict recruit lie to an officer about a past that would get him kicked out of the army instantly?

What Women Should Really Know

A tiny handful of AIDS cases suggests sexual transmission from woman to man, but no such cases have been absolutely verified, and some researchers, noting that AIDS is transmitted sexually through penetration, say without equivocation that women cannot transmit the disease to men.

The statistics tell women plainly not to engage in sexual relations with men who are bisexuals, intravenous drug users, hemophiliacs, or liars. This means women are well advised to look out for themselves. (What else is new?) A woman should know, very well, who sleeps in her bed; keep the list a short one; and until she knows who she might be falling in love with, make it a peck rather than a passionate kiss.

AIDS Does Discriminate

Misguided liberals, with their penchant for applying compassion to problems crying out for reason and hard thinking, aren't the only purveyors of misinformation and panic about AIDS. Some conservatives, for their own ideological reasons, have added to the din. AIDS is a horrific affliction for society, even for those of us who are not at risk, but it is not an Equal Opportunity Infector. If there were ever a disease that discriminates on the basis of race, sex, and sexual orientation, AIDS is the one.

II

• The Surgeon General recently compared AIDS to the Black Death, a plague that killed a third of Europe's population in the 14th century.

• The Los Angeles Times warns, "It will not be long before the pattern the disease has followed among gays repeats itself among straights."

• The columnist Ellen Goodman predicts, "As—not if but as— AIDS spreads through the population, 'no' will become a much more common answer to sex."

These dramatic alarms are well meant. They may one day be genuinely alarming. Yesterday's proposal by the Federal Centers for Disease Control to test more widely for AIDS could help assess the pattern of the epidemic more exactly. But in the meantime, fears that it is spreading into the heterosexual population are just that, fears.

There is no clear evidence that AIDS in the United States has yet spread beyond the known risk groups, notably homosexuals and drug addicts. There is some reason to suppose it will stay confined to these groups for the foreseeable future.

Why has the truth disappeared so far from view? Perhaps because the chief interpreters of the data want them to reflect their own messages.

Public health experts see a unique chance to reduce all sexually transmitted diseases.

Medical researchers demand $1 billion in new Federal spending against AIDS, hoping to refurbish their laboratories.

Government epidemiologists, seeking to protect homosexuals and drug addicts, fear the Reagan Administration may acquire the notion that these are the only people at risk.

Moralists see a heaven-sent chance to preach fire, brimstone and restricted sex. Homosexuals have no desire to carry the stigma of AIDS alone.

AIDS Cases in New York City

	1982	1983	1984	1985	1986
Homosexual/bisexual	269	581	1,025	1,423	1,626
% of all cases	60	59	59	56	55
IV drug users	150	328	571	927	1,061
% of all cases	33	34	33	36	36
Heterosexual (partners of risk group members)	8	16	29	61	87
% of all cases	2	2	2	2	3
No identified risk	1	9	20	20	15
% of all cases	1	1	1	1	1
All others*	23	53	82	105	178
% of all cases	5	5	5	5	6
Total Cases	451	987	1,727	2,536	2,967

* Includes Haitians and Central Africans, hemophiliacs, transfusion cases and those still under investigation.   Source: New York City Health Dept.

With so many experts dramatizing the epidemic, it's little wonder that those who depend on their advice are coming to believe that AIDS is already as rampant as influenza.

Legitimate Concerns

True, there are solid reasons to fear that AIDS may one day break out of current risk groups into the general population. It can be transmitted heterosexually. In Central Africa, AIDS is already widespread and affects men and women equally. But Central Africa may suffer from special factors, like widespread medical use of unclean needles.

In New York, homosexuals and intravenous drug addicts are still the main groups at risk for AIDS. Some 91 percent of AIDS cases come from those two groups. A constant 2 to 3 percent of cases are "heterosexual contact"—the partners of addicts and bisexual men. If AIDS were spreading further, there would be a sharp rise in the "no known risk" category. But this continues to remain below 1 percent. The city believes most of its 65 such cases are members of risk groups but deny it.

Five years or more pass between contracting the virus and coming down with AIDS. So what counts in forecasting is not overt cases but infection with the virus. Of New York blood donors who tested positive for AIDS virus in 1985, 90 percent had previous homosexual or drug experience, or a partner who did. The same is true of virus-positive military recruits who sought counseling in New York. Neither blood donors nor recruits are wholly representative, but these figures do not prove that AIDS is spreading into the general population. If anything, they indicate that the risk groups will be much the same in five years as at present.

AIDS Is Grim Enough

Since AIDS might spread, people should learn how to protect themselves by using condoms and avoiding anal sex. But it would be folly to distract attention from the most likely source of spread, intravenous drug abusers. Homosexuals in major cities have admirably set up self-help groups and informed their communities; homosexuals elsewhere may still need education about AIDS. Meanwhile, the Reagan Administration remains consumed by irrelevant and prurient debate over whether to preach abstinence to schoolchildren.

Homosexuals and drug addicts have borne the brunt of a terrible disease that merits, and now generally receives, the fullest attention of medical research. Hysteria about AIDS may squeeze out a few extra research dollars, but at a terrible cost in false fears. AIDS is grim enough without exaggeration.

---

*"One thing is certain: You do not get AIDS the
way people got polio."*

AIDS Is a
Moral Issue

James K. Fitzpatrick

James K. Fitzpatrick is a freelance writer. The following viewpoint
is excerpted from an article he wrote for *The Wanderer*, a conservative Catholic newspaper. In it, Fitzpatrick claims AIDS is not
merely a medical problem, as many liberals and homosexuals
claim, but a moral problem. He states that homosexuals are
responsible for the outbreak of AIDS. Fitzpatrick concludes that
AIDS can reasonably be viewed as retribution for their immoral
sexual activities.

As you read, consider the following questions:

1. How does Fitzpatrick support his belief that there is a
   moral dimension to the AIDS disease?
2. What, according to Fitzpatrick, does the homosexual community hope to gain by convincing society to disassociate
   homosexuality from the AIDS issue?
3. What is the significance of the Judeo-Christian view of
   sexuality, according to the author?

James K. Fitzpatrick, "AIDS: It Is Not Just Another Disease," *The Wanderer*, August 15,
1985. Reprinted with permission.

Give them credit. There is one thing at which American liberals excel. They are slick. They have a way of putting proponents of traditional values on the defensive. Argue against kiddie-porn and you first have to explain away your hostility to freedom of expression. Try to limit abortions and you are cast as an enemy of women. If you feel welfare in the United States has done more harm to blacks than good, you spend half your time trying to explain why you cannot overcome racial stereotypes. If you supported the invasion of Grenada, you are scolded for harboring that bullying arrogance that leads superpowers to see themselves as "policemen to the world." But if you do not support sanctions against South Africa, you are the modern counterpart of those in the 1930s who "did nothing" during the Holocaust. (Similarly they tell us we should be tolerant of Marxist dictatorships because we cannot "ethnocentrically" assume every society is "ready" for democracy as we define it, even though the government of South Africa is called a genocidal police state because it is not moving quickly enough to a one man-one vote democracy.). . .

What the Homosexuals Want

Perhaps the cleverest example of this dodge can be seen taking place in the current discussion of AIDS. And it is working. Homosexuals and their spokesmen have successfully disarmed those who feel there is a need to bring a moral dimension to the question of how much time and energy and sympathy society owes to those who contract the virus. It seems as if it is only in private that the thought comes up that homosexuals have some role to play in preventing the spread of this disease by changing their behavior. The assumption seems to be that it is primarily society's responsibility to find a cure so that homosexuals can go on with their preferred "lifestyle."

Repeatedly we hear the complaint that AIDS has not attracted the same kind of attention as other diseases because there are "stupid, backward people in our society who think they can see the hand of God in the situation. They think they can read God's mind." Or, "Imagine, there are people who picture a God who goes around like some medieval despot afflicting people with pain and misery and a lingering death. What kind of people would want to worship a God like that!" Also, "God is not a cruel God, he is a loving God who wants us to love each other too." And how about, "God would not have made homosexuals with this powerful drive if he did not want them to fulfill their sexual identity." (These, by the way, are near-to-exact quotes I have picked up without really trying by listening to a few of New York City's radio call-in shows.)

You have to admit: It is neat. An attack is launched against those who wonder about God's will in this issue by those who *assure* us that God could will no such thing. The critics of those who have the "audacity" to interpret divine injunctions argue by interpreting divine injunctions. God can have a voice in public issues when His comments coincide with the enlightened opinion of the times.

There Is Shame in AIDS

Sympathy for AIDS victims has taken some strange turns following the deaths of a few prominent people whose homosexuality was unknown until their passing. . . .

There is shame in dying from AIDS. There is the shame homosexuals should feel for having contributed their infected blood to banks that were drawn upon by the innocent. There is the shame of homosexuality itself. The braying of homosexuals that theirs is an alternative lifestyle has a false ring. It is hollow to the homosexuals and lesbians who preserve their privacy. It is the activists who proclaim their unnatural sexual appetites and so gorge themselves as to invite their own deaths.

It is the flaunting of their perversity that is so distasteful to the vast majority who do not seek to search bedrooms for evidence of unlawful alliances. Although there is conflicting evidence, I lean to the belief that most homosexuals cannot control their sexual behavior. The number of individuals reclaimed for a normal life are few. The very effort to reclaim homosexuals is stormed at by them.

Howard Hurwitz, *The Union Leader*, March 10, 1987.

Is my point that Christians ought to see AIDS as the will of God? No, it is hard to see by what standard one might come to such a conclusion. There is such a thing as divine Providence, but there is no orthodox guideline for us to define whether AIDS belongs more in the category of the fire and brimstone that hit Sodom or with things like polio and bubonic plague, where the hand of God is more difficult to see clearly.

One Thing Is Certain

But one thing is certain: You do not get AIDS the way people got polio. Near to 75 percent of those who get the disease are homosexuals. And the record is clear, the other cases are indirectly related to homosexuals. The drug users used a needle once used by a homosexual. Others receive a blood transfusion from a homosexual, or from someone who received a transfusion from a homosexual. The children who become victims are children of homosexuals or bisexuals or drug users who contracted the disease from a homosexual. The disease is being spread by homosexuals to each other, and, increasingly, to the rest of society.

Those who are responsible for the outbreak are men and women who are continuing to engage with a wide variety of partners in sexual acts that have been defined as deviant and sinful by the Judeo-Christian community for over 2,000 years now. Most other societies have expressed similar opprobrium, certainly the Islamic world. Warnings, punishments, exhortation, ridicule, prayer, repugnance, scorn have been employed—sometimes judiciously, sometimes inexcusably cruelly—to help those afflicted with this temptation to overcome their weakness. And those who have succeeded in overcoming the temptation, or who have practiced their vice in secret with a decent respect for their fellow citizens' deeply felt convictions in the matter, have been able to live as tolerated members of Western society. The prissy music teacher, the fuddy-duddy bachelor, the career military man uneasy out of his barracks world, have all been part of our literature and folklore.

This Bothersome Virus

Those who are responsible for the epidemic have chosen to ignore all this. For them, the Bible is wrong, the Church is wrong. The nature of the sexual act taught by these authorities is a quaint moralism, nothing more. Society is wrong. Their sexual activity is not a sin, not shameful, it is a matter of preference, a positive good, except for this bothersome virus that is temporarily clouding the picture.

Indeed some members of homosexual groups express displeasure with fellow homosexuals who are alarmed enough to call for an end to "promiscuous" homosexuality, an end to the casual bathhouse assignations and "gay" bar pickups. Limiting themselves to one or two "safe" partners is too great a price to pay. One New York "gay" activist in a *New York Times* interview complained that "safe sex is unexciting sex." The man makes an intriguing demand. It is as if Typhoid Mary insisted upon her religious and civil right to work in the school cafeteria while at the same time complaining that the local health authorities were dragging their feet in coming up with a cure for her. If homosexuals want society to attack this disease like any other disease they should be reminded that any other communicable disease of comparable seriousness is attacked with quarantine.

A Punitive Message to Humanity

Homosexuals are demanding the right to proudly thumb their noses at the God revealed to man in the Bible and to denigrate the moral codes articulated to mankind through the Judeo-Christian heritage. We cannot know if the Creator would respond in our era in a punitive manner. But it certainly would be presumptuous to assume that He would not. Whether you are a fundamentalist or not, the story of Sodom and Gomorrah is meant to communicate *something* to mankind.

And it is an attempt by patent intellectual intimidation to label as religious bigots those who feel that they cannot help but note that the AIDS flare-up demonstrates that we cannot simply shrug off the inherited wisdom of Western man on such a crucial issue without paying a price. Even a man who believed in nothing more than the patterns of nature symbolized by Mother Nature would have to conclude that the risk of AIDS and herpes and other venereal diseases teaches us about proper conduct in sexual activity.

> *"Scientists must not be influenced by the moralistic debate. They should consider the disease as if it were transmitted by neutral conduct."*

AIDS Is Not a Moral Issue

Alan M. Dershowitz

Alan M. Dershowitz is a professor at Harvard Law School and has lectured there and at the Harvard Medical School on issues of law and medicine. In the following viewpoint, he argues that conservatives are distorting the scientific information about AIDS with moralistic debates on particular lifestyles.

As you read, consider the following questions:

1. What does Dershowitz mean when he states that scientific information about AIDS is being distorted by personal moralism?
2. What, according to Dershowitz, is the point that conservative moralists want to confirm by associating morality with the disease AIDS?
3. What does Dershowitz state is the compelling reason for government agencies to provide the public with all the hard facts about AIDS?

Alan M. Dershowitz, "Emphasize Scientific Information," *The New York Times*, March 18, 1986. © by The New York Times Company. Reprinted by permission.

The time has come to take the moralism and politics out of the informational part of the debate over AIDS.

Let the moralists and the politicians continue to argue about the social policy decisions that necessarily have to be made in response to the AIDS epidemic. But let the flow of scientific information be unpolluted by personal moralism.

We have all heard exaggerated warnings about the easy communicability of AIDS—acquired immune deficiency syndrome—from moral majoritarians advocating that carriers be quarantined, frightened parents seeking to keep young AIDS victims out of school and opportunistic politicians capitalizing on a national hysteria about a dreaded disease whose sources are easy targets for condemnation.

Concerns of Medical Experts

When Prof. William Haseltine of the Harvard Medical School recently gave his university audience some of the scientific facts about AIDS, there was a stunned silence. "Anyone who tells you categorically that AIDS is not contracted by saliva is not telling you the truth." AIDS may, in fact, be transmissible by tears, saliva, bodily fluids and mosquito bites. "There are sure to be cases," he continued, "of proved transmission through casual contact."

Unlike the conservative moralists who rail about AIDS, Professor Haseltine has no political axe to grind. He is one of the most prominent scientific leaders in AIDS research, part of a team that has already made some important breakthroughs in identifying the reproductive mechanisms of the AIDS virus. He—along with a growing number of medical experts—is concerned that the small amount of scientific light that can now be shed in the AIDS controversy is being distorted by enormous quantities of moralistic heat being generated by the current polemical debate.

Political Opportunists

Since AIDS is transmitted largely by homosexual conduct and intravenous heroin use, the disease has provided a field day for conservative moralists. The former syndicated columnist—now a White House aide—Patrick Buchanan shed crocodile tears over the "poor homosexuals [who] have declared war on nature and now nature is extracting an awful retribution." Norman Podhoretz, editor of Commentary, has condemned concerned politicians "from Ronald Reagan . . . on down" for undertaking a crash program to develop a vaccine: "Are they aware that in the name of compassion they are giving social sanction to what can only be described as brutish degradation?" There is an almost gleeful nastiness to the "I-told-you-so" gloating of some conservative moralists who see AIDS as a naturalistic confirmation of the immorality of homosexuality.

38

On the other side, some gay activists see the public response to AIDS as a political confirmation of society's homophobia. They refuse to acknowledge that some of the responsibility for the transmission of the disease falls squarely on those homosexuals who have persisted in irresponsible sexual practices even after the dangers became clear.

The movement to keep open "high-risk" sex emporiums—bath houses and other establishments where on-premises anal and oral sex is encouraged—plays right into the hands of the conservative moralists. A representative of the Coalition of Lesbian and Gay Rights charges that guidelines for shutting down high-risk sex hangouts "are a publicity stunt designed to take the heat off the state and put it on gay men." She claims that the guidelines "ignore everything we know about AIDS."

Consider the Scientific Aspects of AIDS

The quest for scientific enlightenment in the battle against AIDS has been hampered by the unfortunate reality that the disease is transmitted by morally controversial practices. Scientists must not be influenced by the moralistic debate. They should consider the disease as if it were transmitted by neutral conduct—in the way that polio was believed, when I was a child, to be caused by swimming in cold water.

Distorting the Facts

AIDS has become one of history's classic examples of "blaming the victim." The logic seems to go like this: Homosexuality is a freely chosen orientation; because it is both immoral and an illness, one illness leads to another. Further, the logic suggests, since sexual orientation is a perfectly appropriate way of categorizing the essence of human beings, it is perfectly appropriate to treat AIDS as "a homosexual disease"—in spite of the fact that there are no "heterosexual diseases." Thus, a medical diagnosis becomes a moral diagnosis, and vice versa.

James B. Nelson, *Christianity and Crisis*, May 19, 1986.

Those who have a stake in using AIDS to prove the morality or immorality of any particular life style, should be deemed disqualified from the scientific debate.

If the issue were whether a particular disease was caused by eating pork, we surely would not want the scientific arbiters to include Orthodox rabbis or fundamentalist mullahs who might have a stake in proving the wisdom of religious prohibitions.

We have a right to know the hard facts about AIDS, unvarnished by moralistic prejudgments from either side. We also have the right to hear the painful truth from our Government agencies, such as the Centers for Disease Control.

Understandably such agencies see their role as informing without alarming. But fear of AIDS hysteria—what some people are calling "Afr-AIDS'—should not be allowed to serve as an excuse for understating the problem. As one distinguished university scientist put it: "We outside the Government are freer to speak" than are the Centers for Disease Control, and the "fact is that the dire predictions of those who have cried doom ever since AIDS appeared haven't been far off the mark."

Professor Haseltine has warned: "If you think you're tired of hearing about AIDS now, I can tell you we're only at the beginning." Let's start hearing more objective information so that each of us can apply our own morality to the difficult social policy choices we will face as the AIDS epidemic spreads more widely.

*"There are only three known ways to get
AIDS—sexual contact, blood and birth."*

AIDS Cannot Be Spread
Through Casual Contact

Jared Spotkov and J.W. Anderson

AIDS is contagious. But it is not known how easily AIDS can be
spread. In Part I of the following viewpoint, Dr. Jared Spotkov,
an infectious disease specialist from Harbor City, California, states
that the virus is spread through several specific forms of contact
between people, none of them casual. In Part II, J.W. Anderson,
a writer for the *Washington Post*, describes a study which found
no evidence of casual transmission of AIDS between AIDS victims and their families or close friends.

As you read, consider the following questions:

1. What is the "cycle of denial and hysteria" that Spotkov
   describes? How does he believe this cycle influences the
   public's perception of the contagiousness of AIDS?
2. Neither Spotkov nor Anderson claim that everything is
   known about how AIDS is spread. Why are they willing to
   assert that AIDS is not spread through casual contact? Do
   you agree with them?
3. Why does Anderson believe the Montefiore study proves
   that there is little danger of contracting AIDS in the school
   or workplace?

Jared Spotkov, "Spread of AIDS Casually Is Difficult or Impossible," *Los Angeles Times*,
August 27, 1985. Reprinted with the author's permission.
J.W. Anderson, "AIDS: The One Case Nobody Has Found," *The Washington Post National
Weekly Edition*, August 4, 1986. © The Washington Post.

I

It's a fact that AIDS, an incurable illness caused by a virus, is spreading through our population. It's a fact that we all are threatened, though homosexuals remain the most at risk. And it's a fact that no "magic bullet" is likely to be found soon to stop AIDS. It is *not* true that the disease can be spread by a touch or a glance.

The facts about AIDS keep getting lost in a cycle of denial and near hysteria—denial that AIDS extends beyond the homosexual community, and paranoia that everyone may be infected. Fear and denial both foster the myths that further hurt those who are suffering from the disease and allow us to ignore where the true danger lies. . . .

AIDS is the most serious manifestation of a range of illnesses caused by infection with a newly discovered virus, HTLV-3 (human T-cell lymphotrophic virus, type 3). Technically, AIDS is a condition of increased susceptibility to certain kinds of infections and cancers resulting from the destruction of the most important regulatory cells of the body's immune system. . . . For every person with AIDS, there may be nine or more carrying the virus who will experience either slight symptoms or no illness at all.

This is the crux of the problem: The large number of people who are infected but not ill can pass the virus on to others. In fact, transmission is most likely from these people rather than from those who are ill with AIDS. It is not known how long the infection may last, or how long the virus may be active, but it could be for life.

We know how the infection is transmitted. The most common means is sexual intercourse—either heterosexual or homosexual—through an exchange of body fluid. Since this includes saliva, presumably deep kissing could transmit the infection. Contact with infected blood is another means of transmission. (Our blood supplies are now basically safe, because of screening.) Drug addicts who share needles are at high risk. Infected pregnant women may pass the virus to the fetus; breastfeeding *may* also be a means of transmission.

How AIDS Isn't Spread

By contrast, it is very difficult—perhaps impossible—to spread infection by "casual" contact. . . . No transmission has been reported from passing contact with oral secretions, skin contact or by being in the same room with an AIDS patient. In certain areas of Africa the virus seems to have spread from one family member to others without sexual transmission. However, the details are not known, and this has not occurred anywhere else.

In short, there is no evidence of risk to family members, friends or other caretakers who do not have sexual contact or exposure to blood or intimate body fluids of AIDS patients.

Outside the body, the AIDS virus is deceptively fragile; it is destroyed by drying, by common cleansing solutions and by exposure to ultraviolet light. Fragility notwithstanding, and despite many advances with new antiviral drugs, there is still no effective treatment of the immune deficiency that can result from the virus. Some of the infections and cancers that afflict people with AIDS can be temporarily treated, but, in the absence of a functioning immune system, the same and other infections occur and recur. A vaccine to prevent initial HTLV-3 infection is a possibility, but many obstacles remain before even preliminary testing.

No Evidence of Casual Transmission

Skeptics point out that the incubation period of AIDS is several years. Only recently has there been a significant number of AIDS victims. Who is to say they aren't transmitting the disease in ways that won't become tragically apparent until years from now? In fact, the average time between infection and diagnosis of AIDS is one year for children, two for adults. AIDS has been under study for seven years, and yet not a single case of casual transmission has surfaced so far. What's more, among the 300 family members of AIDS victims who have had blood tests, none has shown the presence of the virus.

AIDS, like other infectious diseases, is transmittable after infection, and not just when the symptoms appear. The people developing AIDS now have been carriers for a long time. If the disease were transmittable in ways other than those that already have been established, this would show up now, not several years from now.

The New Republic, October 14, 1985.

From all the foregoing considerations, we can reach several conclusions: First and foremost, AIDS is not spread by mysterious mists in the street or by the breath and tears of its victims. It resembles syphilis and hepatitis-B more than it does the Black Plague of the Middle Ages. So shunning people who have AIDS does no one any good, and only adds to the victims' suffering.

How To Avoid AIDS

The only secure means of avoiding infection is to limit one's sexual contacts, particularly with people who are promiscuous or who have had contact with other people who then developed AIDS, or who are intravenous drug users. Although the use of a condom has not been proved to prevent infection by HTLV-3, it seems reasonable to use a condom if one chooses to remain sexually active with other people who may be at high risk. By no means should this be thought of as complete protection, however. One should also avoid intimate contact with blood and body fluids, like semen and saliva, of those who are known or suspected to be infected with HTLV-3.

We have come far in our understanding of this disease, but we have much further to go in sparing its victims the unnecessary added pain of ostracism born of myths. Los Angeles' ordinance barring discrimination against the victims of AIDS is a welcome step.

Until a protective vaccine and effective treatment for those with AIDS become available (if ever), giving the facts to our children, friends and loved ones, and supporting research into the virus and its diseases, may slowly halt its spread. But remember: We have never been able to control an epidemic of sexually transmitted disease. So it appears that AIDS will be with us for a long time, perhaps for our lifetimes. We must learn to deal with it intelligently and humanely.

II

AIDS is a terrible disease—painful, debilitating and, so far, invariably fatal. It is also contagious. As it spreads, urgent questions arise about controlling it.

It is a venereal disease. Your views about preventive measures are very likely to be related to your views about promiscuity, and particularly homosexual promiscuity. Although AIDS can be spread by heterosexual intercourse, homosexual contact remains the route by which it most commonly travels. . . .

Transmission by Blood Transfer

AIDS can be transmitted by blood transfer—as in a transfusion, or injection with an infected needle—and by birth to an infected mother. More than 22,600 cases of AIDS have been diagnosed so far in this country, and 95 percent of them can be shown to have been contracted by one of those three routes. The other five percent? Some were people who died before their doctors determined the means of infection. Some were small children who probably, but not provably, got the disease from transfusions. Perhaps beyond that there are some question marks.

The statistics are reassuring, but perhaps not quite reassuring enough. It's conceivable that, one day, a case showing some other path of transmission will appear. There's no way to prove that there's no other possibility. But the most reliable evidence of the virus' path is in the studies of those people who got the disease— and those who did not.

Mike Peters. Reprinted by permission of United Features Syndicate.

Dr. Gerald H. Friedland and his colleagues at Montefiore Medical Center in the Bronx have been conducting a careful surveillance of people who lived at very close quarters with people carrying AIDS, but were not sexual partners. All of these people lived for at least three months, and some for years, with AIDS patients, most of them addicts, during the time when they were infectious. Dr. Friedland reported at the Paris meeting on AIDS in June [1986] that his team . . . found 145 people willing to cooperate, answering long lists of questions and undergoing painstaking and sometimes repeated medical exams. Although they are not further identified in Dr. Friedland's papers, most are obviously the families of the patients.

Safe Sharing with AIDS Patients

Nearly all of these people shared bathrooms and kitchens with AIDS patients. Most washed their dishes. Most hugged them. Some helped them bathe and eat. Many shared drinking glasses and plates. Seven shared toothbrushes with them.

Out of the 145, only one tests positive for the AIDS virus. She is the daughter, five years old at the time of screening, of two addicts, both infected. She apparently contracted the disease at birth from her mother.

Another kind of close-range study follows the people—doctors, nurses, orderlies—working in hospitals with many AIDS patients. Dr. Merle A. Sande reported February [1986] in the New England

Journal of Medicine that at his hospital, San Francisco General, more than 300 health care workers "with intense and sustained exposure to patients with AIDS for nearly four years" have been examined. All test negative for AIDS with the exception of 14 who are homosexual. Dr. Sande said last week that, in the five months since February, that pattern has not changed.

There are only two known cases in which hospital workers have been infected—both nurses, one in Britain and one in this country. Both were accidentally jabbed with infected needles—and not only jabbed, but actually injected with infected blood in the syringe.

In one deeply poignant case, a mother acquired the disease from a child who had got it through transfusion. The mother cared for the child herself with great devotion and refused to wear gloves although the therapy required intravenous needles and the child was suffering from a bloody diarrhea. It seems probable that the mother was infected by direct bloodstream contact through nicks or small sores on her hands.

The Case No One Has Found

All of these studies come to the same point: there are only three known ways to get AIDS—sexual contact, blood and birth. That is why the Public Health Service has concluded that there is no known risk of infection through normal daily contact at school or at work.

The Justice Department's famous memorandum did a real disservice by suggesting the opposite. The purpose of the memorandum was to argue that people carrying AIDS are not protected by federal law against discrimination but it went well beyond that point to imply large and unknown dangers. After quoting the PHS's finding that there's no known risk of infection in the work place, the Justice Department went on to say: "It has been suggested, however, that conclusions of this character are too sweeping.". . .

Society has broad powers to impose sanctions—Draconian sanctions, if necessary—on the carriers of dangerous diseases. But those sanctions have to be justified by a real risk of contagion—not merely an irrational fear of it, but a demonstrable risk. To bar AIDS carriers from employment in schools or restaurants or offices requires that, out of the cases now being reported at a rate of a thousand a month, there is at least one that was clearly contracted through the normal contacts of daily life. So far nobody has found that one case.

46

"Predictions on the modes of spread of a disease should never be made prematurely."

AIDS Might Be Spread Through Casual Contact

Max Klinghoffer

AIDS is a disease that has a long incubation period. Because of this, experts admit that there is much about the disease they don't understand. In the following viewpoint, Max Klinghoffer argues that because of this uncertainty, health officials should not categorically state that AIDS cannot be spread by casual contact. He recommends several actions to protect the population until more definitive answers can be found about how AIDS is spread. Klinghoffer is a physician and a member of the policy board of *The Journal of Civil Defense.*

As you read, consider the following questions:

1. There are studies that supposedly prove AIDS cannot be spread by casual contact. Why does the author find them unconvincing?
2. Why does Klinghoffer compare current AIDS blood screening procedures to tests for syphilis?
3. What does the author mean when he calls for quarantine? Do you agree with him that this type of quarantine is necessary? Why or why not?

Max Klinghoffer, "AIDS: A Viral Pearl Harbor," *Journal of Civil Defense*, April 1987.

Can the AIDS virus be spread by "casual contact"? This is one of the major questions today in the problems of stopping the epidemic. Most research workers in this field today believe that AIDS is NOT spread though casual contact. They cite impressive statistics about the number of "casual contacts" (as, for example, the household in which an AIDS patient lives; or the handling of AIDS patients by medical personnel) and the fact that few, or none, of the individuals in close proximity to the AIDS patient have tested positive for the virus. It is to be fervently hoped that this is correct!

Evidence Not Sufficient

But they have reached a conclusion—a deadly important conclusion—without sufficient scientific evidence. It is known now that the incubation period of AIDS may be several years. Some workers in the field think it may be over fourteen years. AIDS was first described in the United States in 1981. How can we then say it is not spread by casual contact? What can we say if fourteen years from now there is an epidemic of AIDS among those who had "casual contact" with AIDS victims in 1986? Sufficient time has not yet elapsed; only a small percentage of our population has been tested; and our tests are still not perfected. Predictions on the modes of spread of a disease should never be made prematurely—and especially where the disease has a long incubation period and slow-developing symptoms.

There is another problem in the matter of "casual contacts." What is the definition of "casual contacts"? Is it someone who shakes hands with the patient? Or someone who eats food prepared by an AIDS patient? Or someone who uses the same bathroom? And what of an ambulance attendant who is bespattered with the blood of an AIDS patient? If these contacts develop AIDS fifteen years from now, what do we do? Apologize for our premature conclusions? Let us consider an extreme example: that of a young ambulance attendant, recently married. In responding to an emergency call he finds himself covered with blood of the victim. Only two days later does he discover the victim had been diagnosed as an AIDS patient. Does the ambulance attendant continue to live a normal married life? Shall he plan to sire children? Who is there with sufficient knowledge to counsel him about his future? The simple fact is WE DO NOT KNOW. And how much better it would be if our scientific community acknowledged that we do not know, and if they were to defer conclusive statements until we do. And if we based our handling of such cases upon this admission.

It has been fairly well established that the AIDS victim carries the virus in most (or all) of his body fluids. What happens if the food-handler AIDS victim coughs or sneezes on the food he is serving? What happens if the AIDS victim (perhaps not aware that he is carrying the virus) sneezes while he is caring for the injuries of a casualty with open wounds? Some workers in the field go so far as to downplay the risks involved in the needle stick by a used hypodermic needle. What are they trying to tell us? That a lot of virus is dangerous, but a little bit of virus is safe?

Tests Might Be Wrong

We have been inundated with media information (or is it misinformation?) on the subject of AIDS. We are reassured that blood transfusions are "safe" because there are now tests available which indicate if the donor does or does not have the AIDS virus. This sort of information cannot be blamed on the media alone. Usually they obtain such information from "experts" in the field. But with the lack of knowledge about AIDS, perhaps there are no "experts." What happens if a donor has just recently been exposed to the AIDS virus, but his tests for the virus are still negative? He donates blood which is already contaminated with the virus, but a month later subsequent tests reveal he does carry HTLV-III. What do we now tell the recipients of that blood? Is an apology sufficient for a death sentence?

How Much Do We Know?

For anyone who isn't homosexual, heterosexually promiscuous (though, statistically, straights must be extremely promiscuous— i.e., usually prostitutes or their patrons—to be at risk), given to intravenous drug-taking, or hemophiliac, the chances of catching AIDS are less than one in a million—as far as we know.

But how far *do* we know? The virus can lie dormant for years, and there is no telling whether it will soon break out in new categories of people. The public is entitled to its anxieties. And the official experts are oddly willing to let young AIDS victims expose themselves to classroom diseases that, their immune systems being enfeebled, could be fatal: A case of measles could kill such a child. One suspects that hidden axes are being ground.

Joseph Sobran, *National Review*, May 23, 1986.

Further, all laboratory tests are subject to a certain percentage of error. If medical history is repeated, it seems likely that a few years from now we will have tests of greater accuracy, and we will look upon today's tests as obsolete. The Wasserman test for syphilis, developed in the early part of this century, has been replaced again and again by tests of greater accuracy, and the diagnosis of syphilis can now be made with more certainty. But in the early days of serologic diagnosis, how many cases of syphilis went undiagnosed? And, perhaps even more important, how many individuals were incorrectly diagnosed as having syphilis (the BFP, or biologic false positive), and how many were thus stigmatized? How many BFP individuals were treated for syphilis with highly toxic heavy metals? It is an error to make conclusive statements when they may be based upon tests which are not conclusive.

With the advent of AIDS certain serious social problems become much more serious.

AIDS and Prisoners

Although the Bureau of Prisons denies there is any increased hazard of AIDS due to the prison environment, this statement seems implausible. There can be no doubt of the high incidence of homosexual rape. If we consider a cross section of prison inmates, can there be any doubt that our present prison system is conducive to the spread of AIDS? Can there be any doubt that our prisons will become still another reservoir of the disease? There is another aspect to the prison dilemma. When a man is imprisoned (let us say for a non-violent crime) could we be condemning him to death by AIDS? Considering the overcrowding of prisons, and the incidence of homosexuality, are we not sentencing these prisoners to cruel and unusual punishment? Prison officials may say they have not seen an increase of AIDS in the prison population; but they are ignoring the long incubation period of the disease; and they are possibly ignoring the lack of medical follow-up of released prisoners.

Another major sociological aspect of the disease is forcible rape. It used to be a capital offense. Men were executed for the crime. In the liberal climate of today, the offense of rape is looked upon with greater tolerance. "After all," say the liberals, "she was not murdered." The crime of forcible rape is much more serious than many will admit; and it has become vastly more serious since the AIDS epidemic. The victim of rape must now live with the knowledge that she or he may contract AIDS. Rape victims today are routinely tested for exposure to sexually transmitted diseases. But how do we test such a victim for AIDS? How can we assure her/him that she/he will not have AIDS years from now? Can we tell her/him that she/he may safely marry and have a family? In the light of our present knowledge (or lack of it) concerning AIDS, the crime of forcible rape should once again be viewed as a major capital offense and carry a correspondingly severe penalty.

Quarantine Needed

There has been much talk in recent months concerning the control of the epidemic of AIDS. Emphasis has been on "education," and on the use of preventive measures. As in other areas of emergency preparedness, neither of these methods will totally furnish the answers needed for a critical situation. For instance, the drug addict desperately in need of a "fix" is just not going to consider the risks in using a common hypodermic assembly. After all, every time he uses the drug, and not knowing the actual source or the degree of purity or adulteration, he places his life in jeopardy. The thought of a contaminated needle is not going to deter him.

The halfway measures that have been proposed will not be the answer to the AIDS epidemic. What will be needed are mitigation policies and procedures. Sooner or later we must come to the realization that some form of quarantine will be necessary if we are to control this plague. This is not to say that education has no value in the control of the disease. In fact, *unplanned* education has already played a role. Publicity about AIDS has resulted in the change of sexual habits of many people. However, we need to be concerned about the vast number that education methods, for one reason or another, will not reach.

A Cop-Out

Unfortunately, no one knows how AIDS is spread. They know some of the ways—sex, dirty needles, contaminated blood, mother-to-offspring. The statement that there is no evidence that AIDS can be spread any other way is a bureaucratic cop-out.

Scientists said there was no evidence that yellow fever and malaria were spread by mosquitoes until they discovered it. There was no evidence that leprosy was caused by a bacteria until it was discovered. Scientists just don't know. Every listing of AIDS cases contains a category, Unknown/Other—meaning cases which involve people who do not appear to be in any of the high-risk categories. . . .

A few years ago there was no evidence that the AIDS virus even existed and for all we know it may not have. We do know that in a very short time this disease is spreading far and fast and that so far it is 100 percent lethal.

Charley Reese, *Union Leader*, August 28, 1986.

The term "quarantine" is not synonymous with incarceration. There are degrees of quarantine, all of which have previously been endorsed by the medical community and society in general for many common contagious diseases. Unless some very dramatic breakthrough appears in the immediate future with regard to cure and prevention, some form of quarantine is necessary if we are to survive. The government must act, and it must act before the epidemic is literally out of control. Actions must be taken utilizing the advice of those epidemiologists and other scientists who are not intimidated by the political lobby of the homosexual community and other groups. In fact, if given accurate data, the

51

homosexual groups should be the first to support measures to stop the epidemic, since they are the major percentage of the current victims. Again, incarceration is not the answer (except in those cases where an AIDS victim violates the "rules" and knowingly spreads the disease). But AIDS patients should not be food handlers; they should not be in jobs caring for children; they should not be in hospital work which brings them in contact with patients; and they should not be in any occupation which brings them into intimate contact with other individuals. These regulations should apply unless we find out BEYOND ANY DOUBT that AIDS cannot be spread by these modes of contact.

Strong Measures Needed

Should regulations be set forth, there will of course be a great outcry about "civil rights." But if there are, let us say, one million AIDS patients in the United States today, what then of the civil rights of two hundred thirty million of our citizens?

Strong steps must be taken at once, before the majority of our population has the AIDS virus. If not, we shall all become unwilling characters in Edgar Allen Poe's novel, *The Masque of the Red Death*. The first two sentences of the novel read: "The 'Red Death' had long devastated the country. No pestilence had ever been so fatal or so hideous." The novel concludes: "And darkness and decay and the Red Death held dominion over all."

Distinguishing Between Bias and Reason

The subject of AIDS often generates great emotional responses in people. When dealing with such highly controversial subjects, many will allow their feelings to dominate their powers of reason. Thus, one of the most important critical thinking skills is the ability to distinguish between statements based upon emotion and those based upon a rational consideration of the facts.

Most of the following statements are taken from the viewpoints in this chapter. Consider each statement carefully. *Mark R for any statement you believe is based on reason or a rational consideration of the facts. Mark B for any statement you believe is based on bias, prejudice, or emotion. Mark I for any statement you think is impossible to judge.*

If you are doing this activity as a member of a class or group, compare your answers with those of other class or group members. Be able to explain your answers. You may discover that others will come to different conclusions than you do. Listening to the reasons others present for their answers may give you valuable insights in distinguishing between bias and reason.

If you are reading this book alone, ask others if they agree with your answers. You will find this interaction valuable also.

R = *a statement based upon reason*
B = *a statement based upon bias*
I = *a statement impossible to judge*

53

1. We have allowed a vocal, highly political minority to misappropriate AIDS as a moral issue, giving our government leaders an excuse to abdicate their responsibility for the health and welfare of us all.

2. The AIDS virus will not be stopped in the near future.

3. A woman should know very well who sleeps in her bed; keep the list a short one; and until she knows who she might be falling in love with, make it a peck rather than a passionate kiss.

4. What counts in forecasting is not overt cases but infection with the virus.

5. Since AIDS might spread, people should learn how to protect themselves by using condoms and avoiding anal sex.

6. We have come far in our understanding of this disease, but we have much further to go in sparing its victims the unnecessary added pain of ostracism born of myths.

7. For every person with AIDS, there may be nine or more carrying the virus who will experience either slight symptoms or no illness at all.

8. Safe sex is unexciting sex.

9. Homosexuals are demanding the right to proudly thumb their noses at the God revealed to man in the Bible and to denigrate the moral codes articulated to mankind through Judeo-Christian heritage.

10. We are all at risk from the AIDS virus, though homosexuals remain the most at risk.

11. The time has come to take the moralism and politics out of the informational part of the debate over AIDS.

12. We have a right to know the hard facts about AIDS.

13. Some gay activists refuse to acknowledge that some of the responsibility for the transmission of the disease falls squarely on those homosexuals who have persisted in irresponsible sexual practices even after the dangers became clear.

14. The drug addict desperately in need of a "fix" is just not going to consider the risks in using a common hypodermic assembly.

Periodical Bibliography

The following articles have been selected to supplement the diverse views expressed in this chapter.

America	Several articles focusing on the pastoral aspects of AIDS, June 21/28, 1986.
Robert Bazell	"Waking Up to AIDS," *The New Republic*, May 13, 1985.
Susan Day	"My Husband Has AIDS," *The New York Times*, March 29, 1987.
Discover	"A Dissenter in the AIDS Capital of the World," December 1985.
Peter Goldman and Lucille Beachy	"One Against the Plague," *Newsweek*, July 21, 1986.
John Grauerholz	"Breakthrough Near in Search for AIDS Vaccine," *Fusion*, September/October 1986. Available from P.O. Box 17149, Washington, DC 20041.
Lee Hancock	"Fear and Healing in the AIDS Crisis," *Christianity and Crisis*, June 24, 1985.
John Langone	"AIDS Update: Still No Reason for Hysteria," *Discover*, September 1986.
William G. Most	"Punishment for Sin?" *The Wanderer*, March 5, 1987. Available from 201 Ohio St., St. Paul, MN 55107.
The New Internationalist	"Folk Devils and Moral Panics: Myths About AIDS," March 1987. Available from P.O. Box 255, Lewiston, NY 14092.
Rod Nordland	"Africa in the Plague Years," *Newsweek*, November 24, 1986.
Ben Patterson	"The Judgment Mentality," *Christianity Today*, March 20, 1987.
Kenneth Vaux	"AIDS as Crisis and Opportunity," *The Christian Century*, October 16, 1985.
Stacy Wells	"Killer Illnesses of History," *U.S. News & World Report*, January 12, 1987.

2 CHAPTER

How Can AIDS
Be Controlled?

Chapter Preface

"It is incumbent on all of us to make a frontal assault on the sexual revolution. What was once a matter of morality is today quite literally a matter of life and death." These are the remarks of Dr. Harvey Fineberg, dean of the Harvard School of Public Health and member of a scientific panel on AIDS. The panel, organized by the Institute of Medicine and the National Academy of Sciences in 1986, called for a nationwide campaign to fight the spread of AIDS.

Over 1.5 million people are known to be infected with the deadly AIDS virus. The number of actual carriers may be as high as five million. Official forecasts indicate that by 1991 AIDS may be the worst epidemic in US history. So far there is no cure for the disease nor a vaccine to prevent it. However, scientific advances have made it possible to detect the presence of the virus, and individuals can take precautions to protect themselves against it. Controlling the epidemic is the immediate challenge for society.

Several hotly debated issues focus on what methods of prevention will be most effective in controlling the spread of AIDS. Many agree that control of AIDS requires following the Surgeon General's recommendation to educate children as young as eight years old in the ways of "safe sex." Others argue that the AIDS virus could be contained if mandatory testing and tracing procedures were in place, enabling society to identify all AIDS carriers. A few debate the practicality of controlling AIDS by making homosexuality illegal.

Prominent health officials state that AIDS is the nation's number one health priority. Any method to control its spread is likely to be controversial. The viewpoints that follow debate some of the most likely possibilities.

"AIDS victims and all those who have been exposed must be forced to acknowledge the severity of their condition and take responsibility for the consequences of their actions."

Stronger Screening Procedures Will Control AIDS

William E. Dannemeyer

William E. Dannemeyer, Republican representative from California, is a leading proponent of federal legislation to control AIDS. The following viewpoint is excerpted from his congressional testimony introducing such legislation. Dannemeyer argues that the costs of AIDS will be devastating; thus society has no choice but to establish strong AIDS screening procedures.

As you read, consider the following questions:

1. What arguments does Dannemeyer use to support his belief that stronger procedures are needed to control AIDS?
2. Who does Dannemeyer blame for not initiating the appropriate public health procedures to control AIDS?
3. What measures does Dannemeyer suggest society take to strengthen efforts to control AIDS?

William E. Dannemeyer, "The AIDS Epidemic," *Congressional Record*, January 7, 1987.

The United States is experiencing a health catastrophe of historic proportions and an ethical crisis of equal magnitude. Approximately 28,000 persons have been diagnosed with Acquired Immune Deficiency Syndrome [AIDS]. Of that number, 13,442 are already dead and the remaining number are expected to die within 5 years. A recent report by the Centers for Disease Control [CDC] projects that by 1991 the cumulative number of AIDS cases will total more than 270,000 and the number of deaths will exceed 179,000.

Devastating Scenario

In addition, it is estimated that between 1,000,000 and 1,500,000 persons are infected with the AIDS virus and are capable of transmitting the disease. Until recently it was hoped that only 25 to 30 percent of those infected would become victims of full-blown AIDS. However, recent evidence indicates that more than one-third of those exposed to the virus will progress to the fatal stages of the disease and all of those exposed will experience some substantial impairment of their immune system. If this scenario fails to illustrate the severity of the health crisis at hand, there is more.

The AIDS epidemic will result in a profound loss of life. In the next 5 years the number of deaths attributable to AIDS will exceed the number of U.S. military deaths which resulted from World War II. It is a tragedy for any nation to lose so many productive citizens in the prime of life and to bear the societal cost of such a devastating disease. . . .

Perhaps the most disturbing aspect of this bleak projection is that individuals who suspect they may be infectious and some of those who know they are infectious continue to engage in high-risk activities proven to spread this disease. Despite the authority of public health officials to halt this type of behavior, they have declined to intervene, saying that isolation orders or restrictions on sexual activities infringe on the civil rights of AIDS victims.

The issue at hand is not the civil rights of any victim nor of any potential victims, it is finding a way of stopping any and all activities that may spread this 100 percent fatal disease. The AIDS virus does not have rights, and the rights of individuals who persist in engaging in certain activities are outweighed by the rights of those unsuspecting persons whose lives are placed at risk. It is blatantly selfish for an individual to reject or ignore knowledge which would assist him in preventing the death of another. Yet we are faced with the unfortunate fact that many AIDS victims refuse to acknowledge that their actions could result in the death of another. Persons who suspect they may have been exposed are refusing to get tested because they are afraid of losing their jobs, their friends, and the support of their families. While denial and disbelief are understandable reactions, AIDS victims and all those who have been exposed must be forced to acknowledge the severity of their condition and take responsibility for the consequences of their actions and inactions.

Although I firmly believe that the U.S. Public Health Service and State medical authorities should be the entities responsible for setting and implementing these vital standards, their failure to act has left a dangerous void in public health policies and protections. For this reason I am introducing an omnibus package of legislative measures aimed at taking hold of this devastating disease before it takes hold of the Nation.

Vital Preventive Steps

The first bill is, I believe, the lynchpin for altering the devastating course of this disease. This bill will make it a crime for Federal employees, members of the armed services, and those in Federal buildings who know they have AIDS or who know they carry the virus, to purposefully engage in activities considered high risk for purposes of transmission. The penalty for engaging in this prohibited conduct will be enforced isolation for a period of 5 years under the supervision of a public health officer or until a cure is found.

Clear Logic for Testing and Tracing

The operative term for the rest of the 1980s, perhaps longer, may prove to be "contact tracing."

The logic is clear enough. Wherever the AIDS virus comes from, it is transmitted in the bloodstream by sex (or by drug needles). You can't outlaw sex. But you can try to keep the AIDS virus from spreading, by widespread testing to find those infected with it, who become its carriers. . . .

By all means, hang on to civil liberties. But reflect that if the plague keeps going it will sweep civil liberties away in the wave of panic and inhumanity.

Max Lerner, *The Washington Times*, February 12, 1987.

Although I anticipate that this legislation will not be widely enforced, I believe it is important that credible standards be set and that individuals be on notice that certain conduct will not be tolerated by our society. . . .

No civil rights cry can overcome the realities of actions which condemn another to die. Whether by action or inaction, such conduct is murder and must be sanctioned as such. Society cannot and must not condone different standards of conduct for AIDS victims because they are fatally ill. We must show compassion while taking the preventive steps necessary to control proliferation of this terrifying disease. In my judgment this bill will encourage such action.

Prudent Legislation

The second bill I am introducing is an omnibus resolution expressing the sense of Congress that States should enact the following laws in an attempt to deal with the AIDS problem:

Legislation which would require a blood test for AIDS before a couple may be married;

Legislation which would require that partners of AIDS victims be traced and counseled, as is currently done with partners of victims of syphilis and gonorrhea; . . .

Legislation which would require individuals seeking a license to practice medicine, nursing, or any other health care profession to have a negative test result from a test for AIDS, or a test to determine if an individual is a carrier of the virus; . . .

Legislation which would require that all persons arrested for prostitution and intravenous drug use as well as all persons scheduled to be housed in any prison facility be tested for AIDS or for presence of the virus. It is the intravenous drug user who shares needles and the prostitute with largely unidentified partners who are the major avenues of infection. In addition, States should enact legislation which would require that all persons seeking a marriage license must be tested for AIDS or presence of the virus.

Those persons in any of the above groups who test positive should then be counseled about the necessity of stopping all behaviors which could transmit the virus. Ultimately, it would be appropriate for public health authorities to consider court sanctioned isolation for those HIV positive prostitutes who continue to practice their profession and intravenous drug users who continue intravenous drug use and the sharing of needles.

I introduce this resolution with the hope that States will enact such legislation and take these and other prudent steps to curtail the spread of AIDS. Some claim that the States are the only ones with jurisdiction over the health threat of AIDS. While I concur with the assessment that States should retain jurisdiction, I do not agree that States are solely responsible. . . .

Public Health Service

The third bill in this omnibus package makes it a crime for persons with AIDS, or for those who carry the AIDS virus, to knowingly donate blood, semen, or organs. Evidence that the Public Health Service is not pursuing policies based solely on concern for the public health but on political considerations is obvious when one considers the inappropriate handling of our blood supply to date. Virtually all hemophiliacs in the United States and elsewhere who have received clotting factor concentrates derived from blood collected in the United States prior to 1985 have become infected with the AIDS virus. Nine thousand hemophiliacs and 20,000 transfusion recipients are now permanently infected with the AIDS virus. The most regrettable part of this reality is that the contamination of our Nation's blood supply could largely have been avoided if the Public Health Service had appropriately restricted all high risk groups, specifically male homosexuals, from donating blood at the outset of the AIDS epidemic.

AIDS Testing Is Warranted

It's time to admit that AIDS is a plague and treat it accordingly. By 1991, health officials estimate, 50,000 persons a year may be dying from it; as many as 100 million may have been infected by the beginning of the next century. But the numbers, though stunning, should not paralyze. . . .

Testing for AIDS will lessen apprehension and panic. Opposing testing, on the other hand, can only increase resentment and impede efforts to deal with the disease. Identifying victims is hardly an unwarranted precaution, and those who urge a policy of concealment, however justified their concerns, have something besides the general welfare in mind.

The Washington Times, February 5, 1987.

AIDS was recognized as a blood-transmitted disease as early as 1982 and as a disease peculiar to homosexuals, intravenous drug users, and Haitians at approximately the same time. Despite this evidence, PHS recommended in 1985 that intravenous drug users, which comprise 13 percent of the identified cases, be prohibited from donating blood, while suggesting that polygamous male homosexuals, who comprised 73 percent of the known cases, refrain from donating blood. These initial guidelines served to encourage male homosexuals who consider themselves monogamous, to donate blood. At the time these guidelines were issued, PHS knew that the incubation period for AIDS may be as long as 8 years and that a recent Kinsey report indicated that the longest relationship between homosexuals averaged 1 to 3 years, and yet the recommendation only requested male homosexuals who had been polygamous in the past 6 years to refrain from donating. Following the release of these guidelines, PHS admitted that they were a product of compromise between the homosexual community and public health authorities. . . .

The fourth bill deals with the issue of mandatory testing. My legislation would require all federally funded prisons to institute immediate testing of inmates for seropositivity to the AIDS virus and testing of all persons seeking to immigrate to this country. The most serious threat we now face is the large percentage of HTLV-III positive individuals who do not know they are infectious. These individuals cannot take necessary precautions and stop all high-risk contact because they do not know that their status demands such conduct. For this reason we must begin mandatory testing in high-risk situations. . . .

Similarly, testing immigrants for disease has long been the policy of immigration authorities with respect to such diseases as syphilis, gonorrhea, tuberculosis, and others. No country has an obligation to accept immigrants with a fatal and communicable disease and the United States should, as a matter of course, extend exclusion policies to victims of AIDS and those who test positive for presence of the virus.

The fifth bill I am introducing will require all States which receive Federal money pursuant to the Federal Venereal Disease Prevention and Control Projects and Programs or to be used for AIDS counseling and education to set up a system in which State public health authorities are responsible for tracing the partners of AIDS victims, testing these persons and counseling them about the infectious nature of this disease.

Under current law it is common practice for State public health authorities to trace the partners of patients with syphilis, gonorrhea, and other venereal diseases. It is absurd and unwise public health policy to trace persons with a nonfatal, venereal disease and counsel them about the risks of transmission but to fail to take the same prudent steps with persons who may have acquired, or carry, a 100-percent fatal disease. Oregon and Colorado currently have a tracking system for AIDS which has generally proven effective and has not resulted in "driving seropositive individuals underground," as was predicted by authorities.

Benefits to Society

In addition to being sound public health policy, the role of testing in the AIDS epidemic has some positive implications which have been largely ignored. First, testing immediately reassures the unexposed that they are currently uninfected and provides a time and place where they can be counseled on how to remain that way. Second, mandatory testing would give public health authorities the opportunity to better define the actual character and spread of the disease.

At this time there are an estimated 300,000 HIV positive individuals in the State of California, while only 60,000 have been tested. That leaves approximately 240,000 HIV positive people who do not know they are infectious and therefore continue to infect others. The only way to stop this disease is for infected people to stop engaging in high-risk activities and the only way to ensure that these people can be responsible for their conduct is to test them and inform them of their ethical and legal responsibility to contain this fatal epidemic. . . .

This omnibus package of legislation is aimed at closing the voids left by a lethargic and too political public health system. I believe it is urgent that we shift from complacency to action in preventing future cases of AIDS. In my judgment, the best way to accomplish this is to discard the naive assumptions and simplistic solutions which have hampered our progress to date. We have avoided these and other options out of fear of being labeled discriminatory.

The Sobering Reality

It is time to explore any and all options which may diminish the portent of this frightening disease. It is most properly the jurisdiction of the Public Health Service to take these vitally needed actions, but in the absence of prudent management of this epidemic by the PHS it is vital that Congress and the Nation fill that void and mobilize all available resources and channel them into realistic and immediate solutions. The sobering reality is that AIDS is an epidemic that affects us all, and as a society we must become involved in choosing our options.

This omnibus package represents a number of options which, I believe, are vital to altering the course of this devastating disease. I urge Congress and the Nation to join me in advocating actionable, practical alternatives to the current public health policy which has resulted in no choice and little hope.

"We cannot expect people to respond to medical advice if, in doing so, they risk losing their jobs, housing, insurance, children and privacy."

Stronger Screening Procedures Will Be Counterproductive

Henry A. Waxman and Nan D. Hunter

Henry A. Waxman, Democratic representative from California, is chairman of the subcommittee on Health and the Environment of the House Energy and Commerce Committee. In Part I of the following viewpoint, he contends that mandatory screening efforts will fail to control AIDS. Nan D. Hunter, civil rights activist, is a lawyer for the American Civil Liberties Union Foundation. In Part II, she argues that voluntary rather than mandatory testing procedures will work better to control AIDS. Hunter proposes strict guidelines for AIDS testing legislation that will protect both the public health and individual rights.

As you read, consider the following questions:

1. Why does Waxman believe that government proposals for mandatory screening procedures for AIDS will fail?
2. According to Hunter, what is the real issue in the debate over health policies to control AIDS?

Henry A. Waxman, "For Confidentiality in AIDS Testing," *The New York Times*, February 10, 1987. Copyright © 1987 by The New York Times Company. Reprinted by permission.
Nan D. Hunter, "Mandatory Testing and Civil Liberties," memo, February 1987. Copyright 1987 by Nan D. Hunter. Reprinted with the author's permission.

I

Renewed attention is being focused on questions about AIDS testing. Who should be tested? Should it be voluntary or mandatory? Should test results be kept confidential or made public?

Although the test for the virus that causes acquired immune deficiency syndrome has been licensed for nearly two years, we don't yet know its scientific value, and its usefulness is still being debated. Nevertheless, some politicians have proposed making the tests mandatory—for example, for prostitutes, prisoners, hospital patients, marriage license applicants, pregnant women and job applicants.

Testing Procedures Will Fail

But neither voluntary nor mandatory testing policies can succeed unless they guarantee that test results will be confidential and that there will not be discrimination against those who test positive. We cannot expect people to respond to medical advice if, in doing so, they risk losing their jobs, housing, insurance, children and privacy.

Moreover, misuse of testing and test results could damage the nation's ability to study and understand the AIDS epidemic. What we know about the disease we know because homosexual men and AIDS patients have volunteered to cooperate with research efforts. If misguided testing drives these people away, it could only prolong the epidemic.

We know for certain several facts about the AIDS virus test: It does not indicate who is sick or even who will become sick. The test identifies most, but not all, of those who have been exposed to the disease and who are probably infectious.

Tracing Sexual Partners

Since the disease can be transmitted only through sex or an exchange of blood, other than for blood banks the test results are useful only to the individual and to his or her sexual partners. The social utility of widespread testing is to protect those sexual partners who are not protecting themselves. Proposals to find previous sexual partners are dependent not just on the memory of the individual but also on his or her willingness to name names.

A confusing array of testing policies has already been proposed. The Public Health Service encourages anyone who thinks they have been exposed to the AIDS virus to be tested. The agency has also supported confidentiality of test results and has issued statements opposing discrimination against people who test positive as well as people with AIDS. The Justice Department has determined, however, that if the test is positive, any subsequent discrimination is legal and is not the Government's concern.

The certain result of this mixed Federal policy is that all voluntary testing programs will fail. The only volunteers for a test, which might cost an individual everything, would be those who have no reason to fear the outcome and those who are already sick and may need the test results to qualify for the little health care that is now available.

Those whom public health officials most want to test—those who *might* have been exposed and those who *might* be infectious—will stay away.

Trumped Up Reasons for AIDS Screening

The fear of AIDS does strange things to people who should know better. One by one, Federal agencies are trumping up reasons to screen people for the AIDS virus. . . .

The Defense Department claimed it needed to screen military recruits for AIDS because of the need to perform quick blood transfusions on the battlefield. The State Department proposed to screen Foreign Service applicants and employees on the ground that AIDS victims couldn't get proper medical treatment in some foreign postings. The Labor Department's rationale is even more far-fetched. In order to protect the health of trainees at its residential Job Corps centers, the Department claims, mere education about avoiding AIDS is not enough; it must test applicants' blood for the virus.

That's probably illegal under the Federal Rehabilitation Act, which prohibits discrimination on the basis of disability. It's also ineffectual because the blood test will miss those exposed to the virus too recently to produce antibodies.

The New York Times, December 31, 1986.

Without confidentiality and antidiscrimination protections, the mandatory testing programs are also sure to fail. Black market blood tests, forged identification cards, bribery, safe houses and fugitives—all could result from such tyrannical tactics that are in effect a house-to-house search.

In practical terms, the cost of a vast mandatory testing program would be prohibitive. Furthermore, a de facto quarantine of those who tested positive and subsequently lost their jobs, insurance or housing would produce a permanent class of people who could not provide for themselves.

Confidentiality and Fair Treatment

If policies of confidentiality and nondiscrimination were in place, there would be reason to be more optimistic. If Americans believed they would be treated as citizens with rights, they would respond as citizens with responsibilities. If test results were treated as health information and not licenses for jobs and housing, those in danger might volunteer.

We should protect the public health by protecting confidentiality and fair treatment. If the Justice Department does not reverse its position, then Congress should pass legislation that protects against misuse and assures confidentiality of test results.

II

Our nation is struggling to cope with the emergence of a tragic new disease, Acquired Immunodeficiency Syndrome (AIDS). Some of the responses to AIDS have included proposals for drastic curtailment of individual rights and liberties, purportedly to stop the spread of AIDS. The CDC has convened a conference in Atlanta to discuss proposals for compulsory testing of various segments of the population—all persons entering hospitals, applying for marriage licenses, all pregnant women and all patients at family planning, drug and sexually transmitted disease (STD) clinics.

Forced Testing Will Be Counterproductive

The ACLU supports widely available, voluntary testing programs, coupled with adequate counseling and the assurance of anonymity or, if that is not possible, strict protections of confidentiality. The ACLU opposes tests for the AIDS virus which are forcibly imposed. Indeed, for each proposal for enforced testing under discussion, the ACLU believes that the less coercive policy of voluntary testing would work as well or better. In some situations, civil liberties defects aside, mandatory testing seems destined to be counterproductive, irrationally wasteful of public funds, or both.

Most urgently, the ACLU demands that stringent new laws be enacted to protect the confidentiality of AIDS-related medical records and to prohibit discrimination based on test results or AIDS-related conditions. Without these laws in place, public health efforts which are premised on securing the cooperation of persons affected by this disease are doomed. Additionally, federal and state governments must not be allowed to hide behind a smokescreen of debate on testing—a strategy of, at best, limited effectiveness—while abdicating their responsibility to educate and counsel all Americans on how to prevent transmission of this disease. . . .

There *is* a crisis building in the formulation of AIDS-related public health policy, but it is not the tension, so often depicted, between public health and civil liberties—it is the conflict between public health and the absence of protection for civil rights and liberties. As the number of cases of AIDS multiplies, so will the number of cases of AIDS-related discrimination. Many of the discrimination cases result from breaches of confidentiality in the medical care setting—when insurers learn about HIV testing from receiving the bill for it or when employers are told by doctors of positive test results, for example.

It is incumbent on public health officials, for public health reasons, to demand that Congress and the state legislatures pass laws that will make possible an effective response to the AIDS crisis. Americans must be willing to seek counseling, perhaps including the test; to seek treatment if they show signs of illness; and to acknowledge the need to refrain from behaviors which could place themselves and others at risk. So long as any association with AIDS can lead to loss of job, of insurance, of housing and of benefits, that cooperation and thus an effective response to AIDS will be impossible.

Imperatives for Public Health and Civil Liberties

There are four components to the necessary legal framework on HIV testing.

1. To the greatest extent possible, testing must be offered on an anonymous basis. Anonymous testing is the single best protection against discrimination, and its wide availability will do more than any other single policy to encourage people to participate in testing programs.

The Case Against Mandatory AIDS Testing

Why not screen the masses to find and alert the dangerous million?

That was the logic behind the proposal floated—and sunk— at [a] conference at the Centers for Disease Control in Atlanta. The plan called for states to require AIDS-antibody tests for everyone who seeks prenatal care, enters a hospital or applies for a marriage license. Such an approach could result in 40 million tests a year— some of which would certainly turn up positive.

But public-health experts at the conference objected that such a program would not curb the AIDS epidemic. To the contrary, it would concentrate on groups at relatively low risk for AIDS, consuming funds better spend to discourage virus-spreading habits among those at high risk. Requiring the tests might also prompt people in need of care to steer clear of medical help altogether.

Minneapolis Star and Tribune, March 1, 1987.

---

2. Much stronger laws protecting the confidentiality of medical records must be enacted. When anonymity is not possible (as in hospitals, e.g.), records of AIDS-related care must be insulated from casual or deliberate disclosure to anyone not having a legitimate reason to know.

3. By one means or another, we must provide for continuous

access to health insurance. Whether HIV testing by insurance companies is forbidden, or Medicare is amended to cover AIDS-related illness, or special health insurance is offered by the government, we cannot allow loss of access to health care to be the price of obtaining an HIV test.

4. Congress must pass laws to prohibit discrimination based on AIDS or AIDS-related testing in employment, housing and public accommodations. Federal law now prohibits job discrimination based on handicap only for federal workers and employees of companies with federal contracts. State laws are spotty. We must have comprehensive legislation.

These measures are imperative as much for public health reasons as for civil liberties reasons.

"AIDS education for high-schoolers . . . will help prevent not only AIDS but also other sexually transmitted diseases and adolescent pregnancy."

Safe Sex Education in Schools Will Prevent AIDS

Richard P. Barth and *USA Today*

Richard P. Barth is an associate professor in the School of Social Welfare at the University of California, Berkeley. In Part I of the following viewpoint, he states that AIDS prevention requires parents and teachers working together to teach children about making responsible choices regarding health and sexual matters. Part II is an editorial from *USA Today*. In it, the editors argue that sex education in schools is the best way to help children protect themselves against AIDS.

As you read, consider the following questions:

1. How does Barth support his belief that AIDS education will fail if left to parents and physicians?
2. How does Barth suggest that AIDS prevention should be taught in schools?
3. What are some different approaches to AIDS education in schools favored by the editors of *USA Today*?

Richard P. Barth, "Our Lives Depend on AIDS Education," *Los Angeles Times*, March 4, 1987. Reprinted with the author's permission.
USA Today, "Teaching About Sex Protects Our Children," March 16, 1987. Copyright, 1987 USA Today. Reprinted with permission.

I

After some earlier wrangling, U.S. Surgeon General C. Everett Koop and Secretary of Education William J. Bennett have agreed that the country's efforts to prevent the spread of AIDS should begin in the middle-school years. Now parents and educators must find a clear rationale and sensible goals if AIDS education is to succeed.

Fears About AIDS Education

To bolster such support, concerns about the possible side effects of education concerning AIDS, or acquired immune deficiency syndrome, must be addressed. Few can think about teaching sixth-graders about this link between sex and death without having palpitations. The deepest fear among opponents of early education about AIDS is that information about the disease will be taught in a value-free way—that is, homosexual behavior without protection is just another risky behavior like riding a motorcycle without a helmet—and will therefore increase homosexuality.

But homosexual behavior may or may not change with the advent of AIDS education in the schools; evaluation data must speak to that. We do know that the determinants of homosexuality are substantial and complex, and that the incidence of homosexuality has been stable in recent decades. Given the great and tragic numbers of gay men who are dying from AIDS, it is unlikely that a homosexual life style will suddenly develop an enhanced appeal.

The point to be made, though, is that teaching about AIDS as a homosexual phenomenon is misleading and is not the plan of AIDS educators. This disease has a growing claim on the bodies and lives of heterosexuals.

The Other "Epidemics"

The fight against AIDS is also a fight against the other "epidemics" that parallel the AIDS crisis—sexually transmitted diseases, teen-age pregnancy and drug abuse. Adolescents currently contract more than 5 million cases of sexually transmitted diseases annually. Almost 50% of teen-age females will have intercourse before their 18th birthday, and they most often do not practice "safe sex." Intravenous drug-taking is reportedly on the increase.

It is too soon to know whether AIDS education will change sex and drug-related practices that promote the transmission of AIDS. Family-life educators have a growing sense of what young adolescents can understand about AIDS and its prevention, but the efforts are new and the knowledge gap about youth sexuality is large. Appropriate developmental material must be prepared.

AIDS education of younger children has broader goals than teaching about "safe sex." It informs them of the way in which the AIDS virus is transmitted; familiarizes them with means for self-protection against sexual assault, injury and disease, and helps them make responsible choices for healthy intimacy. Some schools are also teaching about AIDS in science classes, since the study of the disease includes lessons in epidemiology, immunology and reproductive health.

The Motive Is Safety

The surgeon general reported, "Many people, especially our youth, are not receiving information that is vital to their future health because of our reticence in dealing with the subjects of sex, sexual practices and homosexuality." The silence, wrote C. Everett Koop, must end. . . .

As the surgeon general said, "The threat of AIDS should be sufficient to permit a sex-education curriculum." And he is probably right. AIDS had brought words like "anal intercourse" onto the network news. AIDS has brought descriptions of condoms and explanations of "safe sex" onto the pages of family newspapers. Now AIDS may "permit a sex-education curriculum."

How much easier it will be to get a public consensus for a message about sex, when the message is that sex can be lethal. How much easier it is to convince parents to talk to their children when the motive is safety.

Ellen Goodman, *St. Paul Pioneer Press Dispatch*, October 28, 1986.

Still, education to prevent AIDS may work no better than education to prevent unwanted pregnancies—teaching it the same way will ensure only limited success. Sexuality education is too frequently taught abstractly and in a way that is comparable to teaching driver's education using Popular Mechanics as the text. While AIDS education for high-schoolers is not just condom education, it needs the courage to inform youth that using a condom or insisting that others use a condom during sex will help prevent not only AIDS but also other sexually transmitted diseases and adolescent pregnancy. In time this will save lives.

The alternative is to let parents, physicians or the kids themselves teach about the prevention of AIDS. Yet few parents are willing or able to provide needed contraceptive information to their children. Many fewer parents would adequately and accurately tackle a talk about AIDS. A recent study indicates that physicians will not get the job done. Only 22% of teen-age girls and 4% of the boys reported that their doctors ever asked them if they were sexually active, despite American Academy of Pediatrics guidelines recommending this from the time a patient turns 12 years old. Peers are a sure bet to talk with each other about AIDS and how it is transmitted, but gambling on the usefulness of such peer instruction to save lives is deadly folly.

Parents and Schools Together

Parents should provide the moral view about sexuality while schools provide the scientific one. The provision of scientific information concerning AIDS is a starting point for protecting our next generation. Family-life education that includes content about AIDS can also assist parents and youths to talk about the disease. The curriculum under preparation in San Francisco has exercises to promote that goal—students practice talking with parents about AIDS.

We should proceed with AIDS education and accept the challenge of learning what information students of each age can use and how teachers can communicate accurate and activating information. Many teachers will find this as daunting as parents and government officials do. They must do their best, however, because lives depend on it.

II

The curse of AIDS has moved a number of state and local officials in a direction they never thought they would go: toward recommending the teaching of sex education in public schools.

School AIDS Prevention Programs

In California, the state board of education adopted guidelines for teaching about homosexuality, contraception, abortion, and other sex-related matters.

In Oklahoma, the state House of Representatives voted to require courses on AIDS prevention—which will include sex education—as early as the fifth grade.

In Hartford, Conn., a state task force strongly recommended education as the best way to combat AIDS and called for frank, explicit teaching about sexual activities that could transmit the fatal virus.

School districts as far removed as El Paso and Boston have taken steps to teach children how to guard against sexual conduct that could give them AIDS.

All these programs include the instruction that sexual abstinence is the best prevention for disease and pregnancy.

This movement, which needs to spread to school systems large and small across the USA, picked up momentum when U.S. Surgeon General C. Everett Koop candidly spoke out in favor of teaching children about sex at the earliest possible age.

Koop has been criticized by neo-Puritans who look upon sex education as a new form of witchcraft. They attack Koop and school officials who encourage sex education as evil, immoral, and against religious values. That is unfair to them; they deserve credit for their courage.

For a full decade, that sort of ranting intimidated school officials who adamantly ignored the tragedy of kids having kids. For a full decade, they piously pursued policies that outlawed discussion of sex in the classrooms and left youngsters misinformed by playground gossip and restroom graffiti.

But evidence mounted that abortion was more and more a method of birth control; that young girls in poor families who could not afford abortions were giving birth to unwanted babies; that schoolgirls were depositing newborn—or stillborn—babies in school commodes, public restrooms, closets, dresser drawers, and garbage cans.

None of that was reason enough to give school authorities the gumption to confront reality. But now that the curse of AIDS clearly threatens heterosexuals as well as homosexuals, children as well as adults, attitudes are changing. . . .

AIDS will remain a curse as long as there are those who think ignorance is the answer. It isn't. Until a medical cure is found, education is the best answer.

"If our children are brought up to believe that chastity is a perversion and homosexuality is normal, . . . not all the condoms in the world will cut down on . . . the number of deaths from AIDS."

Safe Sex Education in Schools Will Not Prevent AIDS

Norman Podhoretz and John J. Mulloy

Norman Podhoretz is editor of the conservative journal *Commentary*. In Part I of the following viewpoint, he contends that safe sex education programs in schools will be as ineffective at reducing deaths from AIDS as they are at reducing teen pregnancies. John J. Mulloy is a retired teacher and free-lance writer. In Part II, he argues that the only way to prevent AIDS is for schools to teach chastity as the best answer.

As you read, consider the following questions:

1. What are Podhoretz's moral objections to safe sex education, and how does he suggest society should control AIDS?
2. How does Podhoretz support his belief that knowledge and availability of contraceptives will not prevent deaths from AIDS?

Norman Podhoretz, "Control Sexual Epidemics with Moral Standards, Not Condoms," *Minneapolis Star and Tribune*, November 4, 1986. © North America Syndicate, 1986. By permission of North America Syndicate, Inc.
John J. Mulloy, "Adolescent Chastity or Dr. Koop's Russian Roulette?" *The Wanderer*, March 5, 1987.

I

Every day, it seems, another public official comes along who thinks that the way to deal with the sexual epidemics of our time—AIDS and teen-age pregnancy—is by flooding the country with condoms.

Condoms as Protection

C. Everett Koop, . . . urges that children be taught how "to protect themselves from exposure to the AIDS virus." He would thus also presumably endorse the movement to distribute condoms in public high schools.

This particular movement is aimed mainly at curbing the spread not of AIDS but of premarital teen-age pregnancy. But here it is a case of two for the price of one. The president of the New York City Board of Education, Robert Wagner Jr., who supports the school clinics that have been handing out condoms as a specific against pregnancy, has announced plans to show a film in the high schools in which the children will be told that, to guard against AIDS as well, "guys got to wear condoms" both during "your standard guy-girl form of sex" and during "the other kind of sex—anal intercourse."

To an American of my generation, there is something at once poignant and bizarre about this desperate return to the condom. When I was a teen-ager in the 1940s, it was as hard for kids to get condoms as it is easy today. Yet in most places premarital teen-age pregnancies were as uncommon then as they are common today. The reason is that there was much less premarital teen-age sex in those days than there is today.

Encouraging Promiscuity

This background surely has a decisive bearing on the debate that broke out between Wagner and Secretary of Education William Bennett.

Bennett believes that distributing contraceptives in the schools encourages promiscuity. Wagner argues that "the best reviews that we know of show that with such programs the number of pregnancies goes down." Yet if these inconclusive "reviews" show anything at all, it is a tiny dip in an astronomical rate of increase.

At a time when sex is out in the open, and when contraception is more readily available and more effective than ever before, can anyone believe that this astronomical increase has been caused by ignorance about sex or by lack of access to contraception? Can there be any doubt that it is linked with the weakening of the moral stigma once attached to female promiscuity? And can there be any doubt that sex education, with its casually indulgent references to "your standard guy-girl form of sex," contributes to the further weakening of this stigma?

As for homosexuality, there too the astronomical increase of recent years is associated with the fading of the old moral and social disapproval. Moreover, just as loosening the restraints has opened the gates to a flood of illegitimate babies, so it has led to an epidemic of AIDS.

There Isn't Any "Safe" Sex

There simply isn't any "safe" sex for schoolchildren. Courses and teachers that instruct otherwise are betraying the confidence that parents and the public have put in them in entrusting children to their care. Schoolchildren should be taught to practice abstinence until marriage and fidelity after marriage, and to expect your future spouse to do likewise. . . .

The November 1986 report on AIDS (Acquired Immune Deficiency Syndrome) by Surgeon General C. Everett Koop contained some strange paradoxes. The report was as notable for what it didn't say as for what it did.

[Koop said that] "early elementary" schoolchildren "who do not yet know they will be homosexual" must be "taught the risk behaviors that expose them to infection with the AIDS virus." How are they to be taught to avoid getting AIDS? Koop's message is mixed.

In one place, he seems to urge that teenage boys be taught they should "not have rectal intercourse with other males—it may result in AIDS." In another part of the report, he appears to urge the teaching of "safe" sodomy by the use of condoms. Koop is out of touch with the real world if he thinks parents will tolerate this kind of "sex education."

Phyllis Schlafly, *The Phyllis Schlafly Report*, February 1987.

Prescribing condoms as a way of fighting AIDS has something in common with relying on them to stem the tide of premarital teen-age pregnancy. In both cases, the assumption either is that there is nothing wrong with the sexual behavior involved that a few little precautions cannot fix, or that even if there may be something wrong nothing much can or should be done to stop it.

This contrasts oddly with the newly censorious attitude toward the other source of AIDS—intravenous drug abuse. It also tramples on two fundamental truths: that individuals are capable of self-control and that the real cruelty lies in denying them the moral support they need in striving to restrain their reckless or dangerous appetites.

Of course, if our children are brought up to believe that chastity is a perversion and homosexuality is normal, then there is no reason for them to cultivate the one or to resist the other. So long as this view of sexuality persists, not all the condoms in the world will cut down on the number of illegitimate babies born to babies, or the number of deaths from AIDS.

II

When contraception became fashionable in society in the 1920s, the Protestant churches caved in on this issue. The more conservative Protestants continued to oppose premarital sex, that is, fornication, while the more liberal ones devised ways in which to make premarital sex a matter of no great importance. It is apparently difficult to accept contraception in marital relations, and at the same time remain opposed to sexual intercourse outside of marriage. For contraception supposedly offers the means to engage in sex "safely"—that is, without having to worry about having children result from it. . . .

A Different Kind of Safe Sex

There is now a great emphasis being placed upon a different kind of safe sex—safety, that is, for the sexual partners from contracting the lethal virus of AIDS through promiscuous sexual intercourse. This is to be achieved, we are told, by means of the condom, a contraceptive device employed by the male. And it is said that parents and teachers must unite to persuade adolescents in the schools, not indeed to refrain from promiscuous sex—that, apparently, is regarded as asking too much of our young people— but in making sure that the condom is employed when casual sex is engaged in. This means, of course, a complete surrender to fornication, its acceptance as something which should be regarded as a regular part of adolescent life.

The difficulty that some Protestants experience in holding the line on this matter is given special underlining by the case of Surgeon General Everett Koop. . . .

Here is a report from *The Wanderer* on what Everett Koop now stands for:

> In his statement concerning the epidemic of AIDS (acquired immune deficiency syndrome), Koop recommended sex education for children as early as the third grade, indoctrination of preteens in 'safe anal sex' through the use of a condom, and wider distribution of dangerous birth control drugs and devices for adolescents (Jan. 8th, 1987). . . .

Yet, as Judie Brown of the American Life Lobby has pointed out, the key prescription of Dr. Koop—the use of the condom to prevent infection with AIDS—is in contradiction to the findings of his own Public Health Service officials on this matter. Dr. Gary Noble, the coordinator of the Public Health Service program against AIDS, has said that, in avoiding AIDS as a consequence of promiscuous sexual intercourse, condoms are between 70% and 90% effective. This means that Dr. Koop, who is presenting himself to us as a compassionate man who only wants to prevent the spread of this deadly disease and is therefore using whatever means are needed to check it, is in fact exposing adolescents to a great danger of death.

Koop's Russian Roulette

The Koop recommendations amount, in fact, to a kind of Russian roulette, in which the chances of being killed are quite high. In Russian roulette, as everyone knows, with a bullet in one of six chambers of the revolver, you have one chance in six of putting a bullet into your brain. In the use of condoms in promiscuous sexual intercourse, with 70% effectiveness, you have almost one chance in three of killing yourself by contracting AIDS. If the effectiveness is 80%, you have one chance in five (still higher, be it noted, than Russian roulette); and if the effectiveness is 90%, you have one chance in ten of killing yourself by means of AIDS. One might level off these different estimates at 80%, which means that the use of the condom can kill you in one case out of five.

Teaching Safe Sex Endangers Children

Information is never neutral. It expresses a point of view. When information is coldly given, the viewpoint is that there are no consequences beyond what the information gives, and the subject is removed from moral meaning. Most sex education in the public schools morally disarms the students rather than giving them moral sensitivity to help them make the proper sexual choices. Sex education belongs at home, where parents convey this moral sensitivity. This is the real answer to handling AIDS and teen-age pregnancy.

To continue the present kind of instruction is an enormous waste. The real answer is premarital abstinence. The "just say no" to drugs and alcohol must apply to sex.

To paraphrase Dr. Art Uline, there is no "safe sex." Teaching safe sex is like giving a parachute with frayed cords to someone needing to escape a falling plane. Sex education fights the modesty and morality endemic to human life.

Tottie Ellis, *USA Today*, March 16, 1987.

Does Dr. Koop really believe that condoms are a satisfactory means for protecting the lives of young people? Can't he think of any better way of achieving the goal of protecting adolescent human life? Or is he quite satisfied to see killed by AIDS one of every five adolescents who are encouraged by his "safe" program to continue with sexual promiscuity? And has he no concern for those others whose minds, saturated with the sex materials Dr. Koop now recommends, will be led to engage in fornication for the first time? . . .

Catholics and Protestants should join together in a common effort to promote the virtue of chastity among adolescents and college students, since it is only by this means that true protection against AIDS can be achieved. It is now quite clear that one cannot engage in sexual promiscuity and at the same time be assured of safety from the physical ravages of AIDS. . . .

Correcting Koop's Error

Catholics and Protestants should undertake a major effort to place in the health education programs of the public schools, not how to use condoms or learn the various techniques of natural and unnatural intercourse, but the sound and compelling reasons for the observance of chastity. There are already in existence materials which serve to accomplish that purpose. At least two of these have been shown in the public schools of the area where I live. . . . Neither of these gives a specifically religious orientation to its presentation, so they are available for use in public schools, even under the strictest interpretation of the separation of church and state.

The goal of this effort should be to make teachers in both public and Catholic high schools aware of these and other materials, and to show them that here they have the means for protecting the lives of many of their students, who otherwise will fall victims to AIDS. In making use of these materials, rather than those of Dr. Koop, teachers will be contributing to the real physical and moral health of their students. What teachers, genuinely interested in the welfare of their students, can resist the opportunity to enlighten them on how to save themselves from the now deadly sex culture in which they are living?

If enough parents and teachers join together in promoting such a program, perhaps even Everett Koop might be converted. He might then awaken to the enormous error of the sex education that he is promoting, which will lead to death for many of the pupils subjected to its influence. Chastity is not only a moral good, it is also the most practical means to save students from this devastating sexual epidemic.

"[The Administration] needs to declare war on the homosexual culture, revoking its license to kill."

Homosexuality Should Be Banned To Control AIDS

David A. Noebel, Paul Cameron, and Wayne C. Lutton

AIDS is described by some as the end product of the tolerance toward homosexuality that developed in the 1960s. According to the authors of the following viewpoint, in order to control AIDS the government must lead the way in condemning homosexuality and returning the nation to traditional attitudes concerning sex. David A. Noebel is president of Summit Ministries, Manitou Springs, Colorado; Wayne C. Lutton is director of Summit Research Institute; Paul Cameron is president of the Institute for the Scientific Investigation of Sexuality, Lincoln, Nebraska.

As you read, consider the following questions:

1. Do the authors believe the government's policy on AIDS is "free of value judgments"?
2. Why, according to the authors, must a society maintain certain moral norms if it is to survive? In their opinion, how has our society failed to do this? What do they say are the consequences of this failure?
3. What are some of the policies the authors suggest the government can implement to restrict homosexuality?

David A. Noebel, Paul Cameron, and Wayne C. Lutton, "AIDS Warning, The Surgeon General's Report May Be Hazardous to Your Health," *The New American*, January 19, 1987. Reprinted with permission.

Early in 1986 President Ronald Reagan promised that his Surgeon General would prepare an unbiased, factual report on AIDS, including a strategy for protecting the public health.

Everyone already knew that the bulk of the media and the professional and liberal political organizations were advocates and defenders of the sexual liberation movement—including sodomy. But Surgeon General C. Everett Koop was appointed by what is reputed to be the most conservative administration in recent history. Which way would he tilt? In which camp would he unfurl his flag? . . .

Homosexuality Not Condemned

While Dr. Koop muses that AIDS might bring an end to the sexual revolution, he deftly avoids the immorality of homosexuality. Instead, he consistently treats homosexuality as a respectable "alternative" lifestyle. Thankfully, he does advise teenage girls to say "no" to drugs and sex, he does advise teenage boys to avoid "rectal intercourse," and he does advise individuals to avoid promiscuous sexual practices. But the overwhelming emphasis of the *Report* is the need for "safe" sodomy and fornication—not exactly "value-free" concepts in spite of the Surgeon General's claim that his *Report* was "devoid of value judgments."

"As a health officer," he says, "I am opposed to the use of illicit drugs." Nowhere does he say, however, "I am opposed to homosexuality."

"I have seen," says Dr. Koop, "the devastation that follows the use of illicit drugs." But he just can't bring himself to say, "I have seen the devastation that follows the practice of illegal homosexuality." (Sodomy is considered a "crime against nature" in half the states in the United States.)

At the beginning of the AIDS epidemic, says Dr. Koop, "many Americans had little sympathy for people with AIDS. The feeling was that somehow people from certain groups 'deserved' their illness. Let us put those feelings behind us."

Putting such "feelings" behind us is not easy, especially when one watches a loved one dying of AIDS contracted through contaminated blood. Besides, one look at the decadent homosexual and drug lifestyles and most would agree that disease and death are among their natural consequences. Promiscuous heterosexuals knowingly risk acquiring herpes, gonorrhea, and syphilis. One still reaps what one sows. . . .

Regulate *All* Risk Groups

Dr. Koop distorts the situation by arguing: "We are fighting a disease, not people. . . . The country must face this epidemic as a unified society. We must prevent the spread of AIDS while at the same time preserving our humanity and intimacy." Are we "fighting chemicals, not people" with drug abuse? What is meant by "preserving our humanity and intimacy"—that suppressing homosexuality is inhumane? Is suppression of drug abuse and prostitution similarly inhumane? How are we unified with drug abusers and homosexuals? Is homosexual intimacy worth risking death? For the first time in history homosexuals are rapidly scouring the world for sexual partners. What kind of intimacy are we to have with them?

Dr. Koop's pro-homosexual bias is especially puzzling since drug abusers have a better record of slowing the spread of AIDS. In the December 1, 1986 federal Centers for Disease Control (CDC) *AIDS Weekly Surveillance Report*, drug abusers continued their decline as a fraction of total U.S. AIDS cases at a more rapid rate than homosexuals did.

True Compassion

The truth is that the abolition of the laws against sodomy has contributed mightily to the spread of AIDS. The abolition of such laws permitted the exponential growth of homosexual conduct—as illustrated by the proliferation of bath houses in San Francisco—and this conduct has had dire results. . . .

Some "experts" still find it unthinkable that citizens should be hindered by appropriate laws from indulging their impulses, however dangerous such indulgence may be to the entire community. To advocate legal prohibition of homosexual conduct is to lack compassion. True compassion must consider the plight of thousands who will be affected and infected as a result of such conduct. . . .

The obvious lesson is—*homosexual conduct must be minimized by every possible means*. This includes legislation, quarantine, education, social pressure, morality, and spirituality. This is true compassion.

Fred Schwarz, *Christian Anti-Communism Crusade*, October 15, 1985.

Likewise his bias is puzzling since prostitutes (whom he condemns) are implicated in only two to three percent of the AIDS cases and IV drug abusers (whom he condemns) are implicated in approximately 20 percent of the cases, whereas homosexuals are implicated not only in starting the AIDS crisis but account for at least 75 percent of the total cases. Yet, Dr. Koop does not condemn or even criticize them.

Those who started the AIDS problem, who have contributed three-quarters of the cases, get off scot free! These are the ones Dr. Koop implores us not to discriminate against, whose actions we are not to condemn, since we are to be "unified" with them. . . .

It is Dr. Koop's failure to censor impartially these three high risk groups that is placing the nation at risk. . . .

Experts agree unanimously that AIDS is transmitted largely by homosexual behavior and intravenous drug use. "Men who have sexual relations with other men are especially at risk," says Dr. Koop. "About 70 percent of AIDS victims throughout the country are male homosexuals and bisexuals.". . .

In the past, once the source of an epidemic was identified, the information led public health authorities to map out a counterstrategy. But these are not normal times. Homosexual activists are well-organized and well-financed, possessing links to both major political parties. They have strong media influence (Gay Media Task Force) and strong medical ties. When a virologist was confronted with the evidence that anal sex activity was implicated in the majority of the known cases of AIDS in the U.S., he shouted, "You're not helping your country at all by focusing on that."

"The spirit of the age," says Jeffrey Hart, "regards disapproval of homosexuality as simply bigotry, and the liberal mentality is zealous in its efforts to protect homosexuals from any disagreeable consequences of their practices whether social, economic, or medical consequences." Any suggestions that would curb homosexual activity in the name of sound medical procedure are immediately attacked. *Chicago Tribune* columnist Joan Beck went right to the heart of the matter when she remarked: "To avoid taking the public health measures that would be taken if the highest risk group were not homosexuals is already turning out to be a deadly mistake."

Miss Beck is implying that AIDS has become history's first politically protected disease. No other disease in history with the potential of destroying millions of lives has been handled the way government health authorities are treating AIDS. If we had fought yellow fever and malaria the way we are "fighting" AIDS, we would have given "civil rights" to mosquitoes. It is an unconscionable situation. . . .

Strike at Its Source

To subdue AIDS, we must strike at its source: the homosexual and drug cultures. The Reagan Administration has already declared war on the drug culture. It needs to declare war on the homosexual culture, revoking its license to kill. Since the Surgeon General has already determined that smoking and drug abuse are bad for the nation's health, the public has a right to know why the Surgeon General has not added homosexuality to the list. "In a healthy society," says Patrick J. Buchanan, "[homosexuality] will be contained, segregated, controlled and stigmatized."

The *Koop Report* obviously does not accept this definition of what constitutes a healthy society. It speaks of "homosexual couples" and the need for children to be taught how to engage in "safe" homosexual practices.

This *Report* places the government's stamp of approval upon a lifestyle whose values and behavior are inimical to the best interests of heterosexual society and sends an erroneous message to both homosexuals and heterosexuals. It tells the homosexual that his sexual behavior is acceptable with some minor refinements, and it tells the heterosexual that there is nothing inappropriate with "safe" homosexual behavior. Both messages are wrong. . . .

Homosexual Activities Lead to Disease

No one can ignore the connection between homosexual activity and AIDS, and the efficacy of the gay liberation movement in obscuring the reality of that connection. The reader will find that connection not at all surprising, in view of the . . . injuries and bloodletting that are a routine part of homosexual activity. What do they expect, when they do the things they do to each other?

Homosexual activity really is contrary to nature. The natural law is the story of how things work. It should not be surprising, therefore, that the usual activities of homosexuals lead to disease.

Charles E. Rice, *Reflections*, Fall 1986.

How did our nation arrive at this unhealthy condition? The answer is quite simple: We listened to and heeded the Sigmund Freuds telling us about "the dire effects of suppressed desire." We allowed the social Darwinists to undermine our moral nature. We applauded the Fromms, Rogerses, and Maslows for stressing the "Self." We overlooked historian J.A. Froude's insight: "One lesson, and one lesson only, history may be said to repeat with distinctness . . . the world is built somehow on moral foundations." And we forgot historian Will Durant's advice:

No one man, however brilliant or well-informed, can come in one lifetime to such fullness of understanding as to safely judge and dismiss the customs or institutions of his society, for these are the wisdom of generations after centuries of experiment in the laboratory of history. A youth boiling with hormones will wonder why he should not give full freedom to his sexual desires; and if he is unchecked by custom, morals, or laws, he may ruin his life before he matures sufficiently to understand that sex is a river of fire that must be banked and cooled by a hundred restraints if it is not to consume in chaos both the individual and the group.

Unfortunately, government health officials, including the Surgeon General, are ignoring the moral implications of homosexuality and its progeny, AIDS. Dr. Robert Dowdle of the Centers for Disease Control (CDC) declares: "This is not a question of morality. It's just a biological fact." Dr. James Curran of the CDC echoes the same line: "The American public can help by recognizing AIDS not as a moral or homosexual problem, but as a deadly, sexually transmitted disease that is affecting increasing numbers of heterosexuals." For these government officials, morality is not involved in this "sexually transmitted disease." However, we don't believe that we can separate homosexual decadence and AIDS any more than we can separate herpes and decadent heterosexuality.

Indeed, AIDS is just one consequence of our abandonment of traditional values and our adoption of the decadent values of the sex liberators. Every person afflicted with AIDS is a casualty of this sexual revolution (hemophiliacs and blood recipients are innocent victims)—a revolution insistently waged against traditional moral values, which were considered "boring," "restrictive," "uncreative," and lacking "novelty."

Our society is in harm's way from AIDS because, as George Gilder points out, the "liberal journalists, compassionate churchmen, tolerant sociologists, pliable psychologists, pandering politicians, and value-free sex educationists . . . condoned the most extreme homosexual behavior as an accepted life-style." . . .

Towards an AIDS-Free Zone

We do not believe the AIDS plague will be stopped without serious consideration being given to the moral dimensions of the problem. If homosexuality continues to be sheltered and protected, it is certain that so many new germs will emerge that all the science and condoms in the world will not be able to protect us. So what can we do?

Our public health authorities must be made to realize that their first responsibility is to protect the public's health, not the perceived "civil rights" of homosexuals or drug abusers. The U.S. Supreme Court, following centuries of historical and legal precedent, has ruled (Bowers v. Hardwick) that sodomy is not protected by the Constitution. . . .

In a letter to Dr. Koop, Congressman William Dannemeyer (R-CA) pointed out the hypocrisy of some states regarding disease control. He wrote: "In California, if you have a curable, communicable venereal disease such as syphilis or gonorrhea, you commit a crime when you have sexual relations. If you, on the other hand, have a non-curable, communicable venereal disease such as AIDS or the virus for AIDS, there is no proscription on your conduct at all."

The Surgeon General must make it clear that he finds intravenous drug abuse, prostitution, and homosexual activity dangerous to the public health. Thus far, Dr. Koop has condemned only smoking, prostitution, and drug abuse. Upon what basis has he determined that smoking, prostitution, and drug abuse, but not homosexuality, are bad for our health?

Homosexuality and drug abuse have cost the lives of thousands of Americans. It must be our policy to put a stop to both. The intent of our actions must be to make the United States an AIDS-free zone. Homosexuality and drug abuse should be made a violation of both federal and state law. . . .

Criminal Naivete

Can a rational society possibly expect prudence and self-control from a group [homosexuals] *characterized by neither?* If we were confronted by a mere nuisance, a bothersome but easily remedied condition, such misplaced confidence might be tolerable.

With AIDS, however, our society is facing a currently incurable, invariably fatal disease. Its containment ultimately depends on public health officials' ability to modify human behavior. *It is criminal naivete to place our public health and safety in the hands of those whose identity has been defined by their flagrant rejection of social convention.*

Jay V. Garriss, *AIDS: Civil Rights or Civil Wrongs*, 1986.

The Surgeon General must insist that every drug-gallery and every homosexual bar and bath be closed immediately. [In 1986] the American Medical Association recommended that these institutions be "closed or controlled." No federal, state, or municipal money should be given to any homosexual or drug group or organization for any purpose whatsoever. This is a scandal of major proportions, and it has led Dr. John Wettergreen to remark: "So far the chief beneficiaries of AIDS have been the vast variety of homosexual organizations. These have responded to the increase of federal money from $12 million to $140 million in two years for virtually anything connected with the disease."

The return on our money has been recorded for us by [homosexual author] Dennis Altman: "Luckily, much of the information made available by AIDS organizations [funded in part by the U.S. Government] implicitly accepted that gay men would continue to have multiple partners and urged caution in 'exchanging bodily fluids.'"

Two percent of total federal funding for the year should be forfeited, for each week in violation, by any state, municipality, or institution of higher learning that: (a) permits a homosexual bar or bath or IV shooting gallery, (b) declares or enforces "gay rights" or "drug abusers' rights," (c) provides support (office space, etc.) for any pro-drug use or pro-homosexual club or organization,

(d) permits or allows homosexual marriage, or (e) permits an open homosexual, drug abuser, or prostitute to receive payment for services of any kind.

We insist that no open homosexual, drug abuser, or prostitute serve on any government committee having to do with AIDS policy. . . .

Return to Traditional Values

Instead of placing the emphasis on spending billions of taxpayers' dollars on trying to discover a vaccine, which may well be impossible to perfect due to the rapid mutation of the disease, we must concentrate our efforts on Dr. James O. Mason's basic point: "We could stop transmission of this disease today if only homosexuals (and intravenous drug users) were willing to observe certain precautions."

AIDS is a symptom of the immorality that plagues our civilization. Trying to cure AIDS while ignoring the cause would be no different than trying to cure a high fever while ignoring the infection that caused it. . . .

We believe the adoption of these . . . proposals will slow and possibly avert the AIDS crisis. Further, adoption of these proposals will protect us from new AIDS-like germs and invigorate our society. Had the U.S. not abandoned the morality of our ancestors, thousands of Americans would not be dying of AIDS today.

We must recover our moral birthright. We must return to traditional Western sexual values. In the past, by being prudent, we have defeated numerous plagues and diseases. We can be as successful with AIDS.

"Societal discrimination against gay people slows up the battle against AIDS."

Homosexuality Should Be Legalized To Control AIDS

Dan E. Beauchamp

Most public health officials agree that homosexual males play an important role in the control of AIDS. In the following viewpoint, Dan E. Beauchamp, a professor of health policy and administrative medicine at the University of North Carolina at Chapel Hill, argues that to discourage casual, unprotected sex among homosexuals, society must legalize homosexuality and legitimize homosexual cohabitation, thereby encouraging enduring relationships.

As you read, consider the following questions:

1. What similarities does the author find between AIDS and drunk driving?
2. What does Beauchamp think is wrong with current Public Health Service guidelines for avoiding AIDS?
3. According to the author, in what two ways do sodomy laws hinder the fight against AIDS?
4. What does the author mean when he says public health officials should be "building and strengthening both equality and community"?

Dan E. Beauchamp, "Morality and the Health of the Body Politic," *The Hastings Center Report*, December 1986. Reproduced by permission. © The Hastings Center.

The Acquired Immunodeficiency Syndrome (AIDS) is clearly a public threat. The view that it is also a threat to the majority's values is a form of legal moralism. Like public health, legal moralism relies on the use of law and regulation to promote community aims. But legal moralism restricts liberty as a defense against a moral rather than a physical harm. It uses law to protect the majority's morality from the deviant group. . . .

Legal Moralism

In recent times this view has been most forcefully stated by Lord Patrick Devlin in his critique of the 1957 British Wolfenden Report—the Report of the Committee on Homosexual Offences and Prostitution—which recommended removing criminal sanctions for private homosexual conduct between consenting adults. Devlin said: "What makes a society of any sort is community of ideas, not only political ideas but also ideas about the way its members should behave and govern their lives; these latter ideas are its morals. . . . [W]ithout shared ideas on politics, morals and ethics no society can exist. . . . For society is not something that is kept together physically; it is held by the invisible bonds of common thought." Moralism binds the community tightly within a narrow and precise morality. Moralism seeks to purify the community, dividing the citizenry into the wheat and the chaff. . . .

The most powerful objections to moralism lie in disputing two claims often made on its behalf. According to the first thesis, if a common morality is shared by a majority, this alone is sufficient justification to include it in the criminal law. The second thesis is that because a common morality holds a society together, legal moralism is justified on the grounds of self-preservation. But to opponents of legal moralism, serious restrictions on liberty cannot rest solely on appeals to tradition, even when backed by majority approval. Furthermore, there is no evidence that violations of the majority's moral norms, like homosexuality, threaten the existence of society.

The most potent challenge to legal moralism is its frequent collision with a more widely shared value—public health. Restrictions on liberty to promote the public health—paternalism—are today more widely accepted than legal moralism. The trend seems to be, at least over the long run, toward rejecting tightly bounded moral codes in favor of loosely bounded restrictions that promote the public health as a common good. By permitting the majority the right to enforce legally its traditional prejudices, particularly in the sexual realm, the health and safety of the public can be directly threatened.

AIDS mainly strikes two groups—gay men and intravenous drug users—who under normal circumstances are shunned by the larger society. . . .

91

Our best weapon against AIDS would be a public health policy resting on the right to be different in fundamental choices and the democratic community as "one body" in matters of the common health. This new policy would mean the right of every individual to fundamental autonomy, as in abortion and sexual orientation, while viewing health and safety as a common good whose protection (through restrictions on liberty) promotes community and the common health. The public health policy would reject moralism as a threat to the right of each individual, including gays, to fundamental autonomy and also as a threat to the common health.

No Opportunities for Stable Relationships

[An AIDS patient] is quoted as saying that there is a "Catch-22" in society's perception of gays. "It says because homosexuals are promiscuous, immature, and incapable of forming stable relationships, they are therefore forbidden the legal, theological, and social opportunities to establish them." On the other hand, he continues, many straight people "who decry promiscuity are equally contemptuous of gay love relationships that are monogamous. They don't draw distinctions."

Ann Giudici Fettner and William Check, *The Truth About AIDS*, 1985.

AIDS, at least in developed countries, does not seem to behave like a typical infectious disease, which spreads rapidly or easily. Until a vaccine is developed, AIDS will resemble drunk driving or cigarette smoking more than diphtheria or malaria; that is, mortality will rise to a high and stubborn level, which will prove very difficult to reduce. And, as in drunk driving, we will be strongly tempted to use the criminal law to punish the offender rather than to explore the roots of the disease, because the roots of the problem lie in American practices generally.

Education Our Only Hope

AIDS policy must begin with a realistic admission that, given the poor prospects for developing a vaccine in the immediate future, there is little hope for elimination of the disease. We can only hope to control the rate of increase among high-risk groups, and to prevent the spread into other groups. By how much we can't say for sure, but reducing the incidence of AIDS by one-half seems an almost utopian goal. Hence, neither quarantine nor isolation can be the principal path to conquering AIDS. Education is our only hope for prevention, and here we confront the barrier of societal practices regarding homosexuality.

The Public Health Service guidelines to reduce the risk of contracting or transmitting AIDS stress eliminating sex with strangers and anal intercourse, and urge the use of condoms at all times. Gay groups have strongly criticized these guidelines, because their global character seems to imply that the main sexual activities of gay men are, by definition, risky. Discouraging anal intercourse, sex with strangers, or almost any sexual activity that is stimulating with those suspected of being exposed to HIV virus, does seem unrealistic. In many states and localities the publication of such guidelines might provide grounds for criminal charges. Sodomy statutes and other laws against homosexuality serve as a powerful brake on the most potent weapon we have against AIDS—the use of a vigorous public education campaign.

Sodomy Laws Won't Stop AIDS

Societal discrimination against gay people slows up the battle against AIDS in two ways. It threatens their health directly, and it impedes changes in gay sexual practices that heighten the risk of AIDS.

The laws against homosexuality in about half the states, as well as continuing social prejudice, prevent public health agencies from developing and aggressively carrying out frank and open sex education campaigns for safer homosexual sex, as well as frustrating prompt medical attention as a part of an overall prevention strategy. We already have ample evidence that this will occur. In the case of the federal government's recent solicitation for "Innovative Projects for AIDS Risk Reduction," the federal government requires that a program review panel, the majority of whom are not the members of at-risk groups, should review program materials to determine that the general public is not offended by sexually explicit material. Federal officials obviously became jittery that successful applicants might draw the ire of opposed groups and even lawsuits, based on state sodomy statutes.

Many might conclude that, because some media and some locales permit rather extensive and public discusson of gay sexuality, these statutes are not a serious problem. While some media carry rather explicit information about "safe sex," the details of such practices are not widely publicized. It is very difficult in many areas in the U.S. to assure that these data are widely disseminated and that homosexuals can freely debate and discuss critical changes in their practices. Where openness is the rule, evidence seems to show a dramatic decline in at-risk sex.

The sodomy statutes also contribute to the poor health of many gays by discouraging their seeking prompt medical advice and treatment for many sexually transmitted diseases (STDs). The high rate of STDs among homosexual males may increase the risk that those who become infected will develop symptoms or become full-blown AIDS cases. The same might well be true for gay men using drugs of various kinds to increase sexual stimulation. Antisodomy statutes and fear of prosecution or exposure discourage prompt medical attention and limit opportunities for communicating clear advice about safer sexual practices. Indeed, the antisodomy statutes may encouage prejudice among the medical community toward homosexual patients.

An Unprotected Class

We must remember that when public health officials propose measures like screening, they are in effect proposing to a population already outside the law that something else be taken away. Homosexuals are an unprotected class, and you are suggesting doing something to this class in order to protect "the public's" health.

If Congress passed laws assuring the civil rights of gay people, or even mandating that all test results be confidential, that would be a different situation. But that is *not* the situation today. . . .

It should be pointed out that most public health officials are oblivious to the true situation of gay people. A while back, a high-level Public Health Service official said to me: "Frankly, the best response to this disease would be for all gay men to settle down in monogamous relationships." This man seemed to believe that two gay men in Omaha could simply get married, retire to the suburbs, and drive their 2.4 cars happily for the rest of their lives.

Gary MacDonald, *Harper's*, October 1985.

The antisodomy statutes and other restrictions on gay men may also make it more likely that the sexual practices of some such individuals remain high-risk for venereal disease and AIDS. If the sexual practices of many gay men are to change, and if homosexual sex is to occur in the context of more stable relationships, the larger society will have to permit permanent forms of gay association and civil liberties that encourage such stable relationships. While societal discrimination is not the whole story behind gay liberation, gay sexual practices may have been shaped in part by societal pressures and laws forcing gay men to associate secretly in bars and bathhouses out of view of the majority community, while at the same time proscribing gay association by cohabitation and marriage. Gay people cannot now marry and are denied many other legal and social privileges of straights. The freedoms to live where one wants and with whom one wants; to make contracts; and to obtain employment in a normal manner are likely linked in subtle ways to encouraging enduring relationships, which lower the risk of exposure to STDs.

Success in the battle against AIDS depends on replacing old im-

ages of the tightly bound community based on sodomy statutes—
"us" and "them"—with a more complex public health policy that
combines the right to be different with the view that in matters
of the common health and safety we are "one body" with a common good. This complex vision, combining equality and community, rests on a double movement; the health of the body politic
depends on mutual trust and a willingness to accept the burdens
of citizenship; these burdens are accepted because a narrow
moralism is rejected and all are equal partners in the body politic,
free to pursue their own ultimate ends.

Therefore, health education against AIDS should involve far
more than disseminating explicit sex education materials. Health
education means building and strengthening both equality and
community, challenging traditional superstitions and defending
the legitimate rights of homosexuals. Health officials should
actively—albeit prudently— seek the repeal of state laws proscribing homosexuality as major barriers to this public education, laws
whose continued existence threatens the public health. Public
health groups should also support efforts to broaden the civil liberties of gay people and eliminate laws that permit employers,
landlords, the military, or commercial establishments to
discriminate in employment, housing, insurance, or military
service.

A Contentious Issue

While public health and the rights to citizenship are a cor-
nerstone in any community, removing centuries of prejudice and
discrimination dictates caution and political prudence. The prejudices against homosexuality are deep-seated and not likely to give
way easily.

Of course, the moralist sees laws against homosexuality as or-
dained by God and tradition. In this view, laws forbidding sodomy
among males and females or partners of the same sex are a vital
bulwark against AIDS. If homosexuality were to decline sharply,
the number of AIDS cases would fall in turn. Guidelines for safe
sex are, accordingly, guidelines for safe sodomy and are, as such,
patently repugnant.

Similarly the moralist is reluctant to distribute sterile needles
to intravenous drug users as a strategy to stop the spread of AIDS.
Drug use, to the moralist, is not just a health problem; it is a
vice. . . .

The same groups that object, in the name of religion, to abortion, to sex education, and to teenage contraception also object
to eliminating the sodomy laws and to expanding the right of
privacy in matters of sex, as well as strengthening the rights of
homosexuals to decent medical care, to employment, housing, and
military service. Public health cannot ignore the blunt truth that

society's restrictions on sexual freedom are a fundamental public health issue. Legal moralism has always been concerned at its core with sexual practices believed to hold together and strengthen the traditional family unit.

Moralists and the Common Good

This is not to say that the majority has no legitimate interest in regulating gay sexual practices on the grounds of morality. Many of these practices may give deep offense to members of the community, much as many features of heterosexual practices placed on public display are offensive. The public peace surely demands reasonable regulation of public sexual practices. The majority seems especially fearful regarding the relation of homosexuals and the young, despite the evidence that sexual molestation seems largely a crime of heterosexual males. Yet prudence seems to indicate that with repeal of sodomy statutes, statutes against child abuse need to be strengthened where necessary.

Public Enforcement a Bad Idea

It has become heresy to suggest that moral questions should be publicly confronted. But why shouldn't a society confront questions of morality?

The danger comes not from debate but from the belief that moral questions are legislatable. In fact, the courts, simply by addressing a moral issue, undermine morality. . . .

Public debate over private morality is not a bad idea.

Public enforcement of private morality is not a good idea.

David Black, *The Plague Years*, 1985.

Moralists believe that certain forms of behavior must be observed if society's central orders—religion, work, family, and relations between the sexes—are to be upheld. Honor to parents, devotion to family, chastity, hard work, and the fear of God are in themselves valuable and should be preserved. But religious morality often becomes a triumph of form over substance. Like those who demythologize superstitions and myths in the Bible, replacing these with the timeless ethic of love and community, the health official must seek to transcend a traditional morality and focus debate on the link between the common good and the equal rights of our fellow citizens who are gay. . . .

In our times, the trend has been to remove the ancient prejudices and superstitions preserved in the antisodomy statutes in the states—twenty-six states have done so. And some locales have passed gay civil rights ordinances to protect against discrimination. Recently in Georgia, a homosexual male entered federal court arguing that charges of sodomy brought against him for acts committed with a consenting partner in his own home were unconstitutional. While the federal district court ruled against him, the federal circuit court reversed, arguing that these cases demanded a more strict scrutiny if they were to pass the constitutional test. In other words, the state had to demonstrate that it had a compelling interest in legislating against homosexuality, and that this legislation was the most limited means available to achieve its purpose.

The Supreme Court, for the time being, has rejected this view. By a 5 to 4 vote in *Bowers v. Hardwick*, the Court upheld the right of the majority to legislate against homosexual acts, committed even in private, on the grounds that repugnance for homosexuality is an ancient and deeply rooted community sentiment. In an earlier decision, the future Chief Justice compared these laws to public health legislation to prevent the spread of communicable diseases. . . .

The decision of the Supreme Court is a threat to the entire advance of the privacy decisions of the past two decades. The work of the Court in trying to untangle the claims of moralism, and the claims of public health, by forging a new equality that combines the common good and the right to be left alone in new ways, has been left dangling. If the Court's ruling is to be reversed, the thesis that legal moralism threatens the public health as well as the rights of all citizens, including gays, must be pressed even more vigorously. . . .

Health Officials Should Lead

Above all else, for both these groups [homosexuals and drug users] we should keep our eyes on the central issue—the many ways in which centuries of religious and social superstitions and prejudice stand in the way of improving the public health. Modern public health rests on a complex equality that replaces traditional restrictions with limits rooted in protection against actual harms. Equating the public health with simplistic restrictions on homosexuality per se will only result in fruitless debates over matters like quarantine and isolation, public health strategies that have little role in this epidemic. Hoping for a technological shortcut in the form of a vaccine is not realistic and can cost tens of thousands of lives, especially if this hope keeps us from facing the task of public education and reform of our laws against homosexuality. These reforms can help prepare the way for altering sexual lifestyles among the gay community. The pubic health community should take the lead and, state by state, demand the repeal of harmful statutes and restrictions on gay life. The health of the body politic depends on rejecting the communal disease of sexual prejudice.

a critical thinking activity

Evaluating AIDS and Public Health Concerns

Margulies 1987, *Houston Post.*

There are many provocative arguments debating how the nation can control the spread of AIDS. One method, illustrated in the cartoon above, is to give out condoms to young people so they can protect themselves against AIDS. Many people take issue with this practice and argue that it is encouraging promiscuity by saying to youth, "Go out and have a good time, and take these with you for protection!"

In this activity you have a chance to examine your values in the area of public health by considering methods to control AIDS and debating them with others in a group.

Part I

Working in small groups, and using the viewpoints in this chapter as a resource, indicate how effective the group believes each of the following methods will be in controlling AIDS. *Use a V for very effective, M for moderately effective, and N for not effective.* Consider only how effectively each method can prevent or control AIDS if carried out exactly as stated.

_____ require all schools to teach courses on AIDS prevention beginning with the fifth grade

_____ legalize homosexual marriages

_____ leave AIDS contact tracing and notification to individual discretion

_____ test all persons arrested for prostitution and drug abuse for AIDS

_____ provide condoms in schools and public restrooms

_____ tattoo all AIDS carriers

_____ use public service announcements to encourage all those at risk to submit to an AIDS test

_____ prohibit AIDS carriers from holding jobs in the health care and food industry

_____ provide free, anonymous, and confidential AIDS tests in all public health centers

_____ pass laws to prohibit any form of discrimination against persons with AIDS

_____ let parents and the church teach children moral values and sexual behavior

_____ make it a federal crime to engage in any activity that allows the AIDS virus to be transmitted

_____ practice sexual abstinance until marriage

_____ require AIDS tests for all marriage license applicants

_____ require annual AIDS test for every man, woman, and child regardless of risk classification

Part II

Using the same list, repeat Part I. This time consider only the moral or social values affected by each method. Indicate the group's consensus as to whether or not each method seems a morally acceptable way to control AIDS. *Mark A for acceptable and U for unacceptable.*

Part III

Consider both aspects of these issues and, as a group, decide which methods society should use to control AIDS. Each group should compare its evaluation with others in a class-wide discussion.

Periodical Bibliography

The following articles have been selected to supplement the diverse views expressed in this chapter.

Lawrence K. Altman — "AIDS Poses a Classic Dilemma," *The New York Times*, February 10, 1987.

Robert Bazell — "Catching Up with AIDS," *The New Republic*, February 23, 1987.

David R. Carlin Jr. — "Not by Condoms Alone," *Commonweal*, March 13, 1987.

Willard Gaylin — "On AIDS and Moral Duty," *The New York Times*, April 24, 1987.

Katherine M. Griffin — "Learning About AIDS," *American Medical News*, March 20, 1987.

Institute of Medicine and National Academy of Sciences — "Confronting AIDS: Direction for Public Health, Care, and Research," *Issues in Science and Technology*, Winter 1987.

Barbara Kantrowitz — "The Grim ABCs of AIDS," *Newsweek*, November 3, 1986.

Carol Levine and Joyce Bernel, eds. — "AIDS: Public Health and Civil Liberties," *Hastings Center Report*, December 1986.

Paul Moore Jr. — "How To Fight AIDS: Bipartisanship," *The New York Times*, April 16, 1987.

The Nation — "Secondary Infection," February 14, 1987.

Rod Nordland — "AIDS: Fear of Foreigners," *Newsweek*, April 6, 1987.

Beny Primm and Mervyn Silverman — "Mandatory Test for AIDS?" a debate, *U.S. News & World Report*, March 9, 1987.

Marcia Quackenbush — "Sex Education May Now Be a Matter of Life and Death, But How Do You Tell an 8-year-old About AIDS?" interview, *People Weekly*, November 10, 1986.

U.S. News & World Report — "AIDS: Should You Be Tested?" April 20, 1987.

Morton Winton and Sheldon H. Landesman — "AIDS and a Duty To Protect," case studies, *Hastings Center Report*, February 1987.

Mortimer B. Zuckerman — "AIDS: A Crisis Ignored," *U.S. News & World Report*, January 12, 1987.

3

Will Controlling AIDS Undermine Civil Rights?

Chapter Preface

AIDS presents a dilemma to those concerned about civil rights. On the one hand, it is in society's interest to control the spread of infectious diseases like AIDS. On the other hand, American law recognizes that individuals, even those with AIDS, have rights. These people should not be discriminated against unless they are a clear threat to others. At what point does society's right to control disease interfere unjustly with an infected person's legitimate rights?

Defenders of AIDS carriers and members of high risk groups affected by discrimination in housing and employment argue that there is little medical justification for it. But those calling for restrictions claim that society must be cautious to avoid spreading AIDS. They are skeptical of the assurances of health officials that AIDS cannot be spread by casual contact, and fear that AIDS carriers will unknowingly spread the virus while working at restaurants or hospitals.

Many who call for restrictions on AIDS carriers also call for legal measures to control sexual behavior thought to spread AIDS, particularly homosexual sex. They argue that this behavior is a health hazard and that it should be criminalized in order to discourage it. But some argue that changes in people's behavior must be voluntary, that compulsory measures will not work. To these critics, enforcing laws controlling sexual behavior is not only an invasion of privacy; it is counterproductive in controlling AIDS since it discourages cooperation with health authorities.

Public health officials and lawmakers will be under increasing pressure to make decisions about legal responses to AIDS. They will have to decide whether or not to broaden and enforce laws regulating sexual conduct. They will have to decide when and if an AIDS carrier's rights to housing and employment should be restricted for health reasons. AIDS is forcing Americans to reexamine how much freedom individuals can have and in what circumstances the public health is more important than that freedom.

"The lives saved through . . . cooperation with AIDS surveillance and research will not . . . be those whose lives are at risk."

Civil Rights Must Take Priority in Controlling AIDS

Cindy Patton

AIDS made its initial impact in the United States among groups of people already considered by many as being outside the mainstream of society: homosexuals, Haitian immigrants, and drug users. This, combined with the fear of a deadly and mysterious disease, causes many AIDS carriers to fear reprisals if they reveal their illness. Cindy Patton works for a daily newspaper in Massachusetts and has written two books on AIDS. In the following viewpoint, she claims that those at risk from AIDS have good reason to fear the government agencies that are supposed to help them.

As you read, consider the following questions:

1. What challenges does the author state AIDS victims face in applying for government aid?
2. What, according to Patton, must members of AIDS risk groups be assured of before they can cooperate effectively with health officials?
3. What consequences does Patton see coming from the failure of public health and government officials to insure confidentiality of test results?

Cindy Patton, *Sex and Germs*, 1985. From South End Press, $9.00 paper and $25.00 cloth, 116 St. Botolph St., Boston, MA 02115. Reprinted with permission.

The U.S. entered the era of AIDS with conflicting demands: enormous cynicism surrounded the very enterprise of medicine, costs were thought to be too high, and medicine was alternately believed to have caused oppression by inappropriately labeling people and to have helped relieve some oppression by pronouncing blacks the biological equals of whites, admitting that women's reproductive anatomy is compatible with work, and that homosexuality is a "normal" difference, not a biological defect. The arrival of AIDS provoked even more contradictory demands from both the left and the right. Rightists claimed that any money spent on AIDS was too much, that AIDS was an elective disease created by homosexuals who might just as well die off. Lesbian and gay activists demanded more responsive funding, and more concerted research, but cautioned their brothers not to get involved in the research until legal issues could be sorted out. . . .

Fear Can Limit Rights, Services

Once it was clear that AIDS was actually an epidemic and not just a collection of cases, emergency care personnel, dentists, hospital support services, doctors and nurses, even undertakers began refusing to get anywhere near a person with AIDS. AIDS presented an unforeseen case for medical workers who had grown up and been trained in an age that did not know the constant threat of contracting a deadly illness in their line of work. Other than occasional, isolated cases, most hospital workers only feared contracting hepatitis or tuberculosis, which might cause a short-term illness, but would rarely be fatal. AIDS created a serious crisis in medical care delivery ethics: the image of the tireless and self-sacrificing nurse, doctor, ambulance attendant, or emergency room attendant quickly gave way as workers consulted with their union representatives and refused to treat patients. Although hospitals and professional associations have developed precautions for handling AIDS cases, many workers simply do not believe the protocols are adequate. Each new medical discovery reopens the contagion question. As long as the researchers can provide data that hospital workers who follow precautions do not increase their chances of getting AIDS, the legal and ethical establishments back up the rights of the patient. What happens, however, when a health care worker *does* get AIDS at the job? Which way will justice wink then?

The conservative police and prison guard unions continue to maintain that they should not be forced to work with people who might even be suspected of having ("harboring" is the term they generally use) AIDS. The lack of any clear knowledge about who has or might be at risk for AIDS made it immediately evident that these elective injunctions could be construed to include anyone who even *looked* gay, Haitian, or like a prostitute or drug user.

Although the medical professionals have uneasily gone back on the job, there are still occasional stories of indigent people left untreated or AIDS patients in hospitals left for several shifts lying in their full bedpans, having their food left at the door, or being shipped off to other care facilities. . . .

Lesbian/gay rights advocates and lawyers set to work, often behind the scenes, to make sure that workers used the precautions dictated by their professional associations. There were two lines of attack used to insure access to services: existing civil rights statutes that included sexual preference, and existing disability laws. . . .

A New Class of Lepers

Evidence of a trend toward widespread legal discrimination against persons suspected of AIDS or AIDS-related complex (ARC) could result in almost as devastating an effect on the lives of other marginalized segments of our society as the physical manifestations of the disease. . . .

Talk of mandatory [HIV] screening raises particular concern among Blacks and other minorities who would most be affected—food handlers, those who work in child care and other personal service jobs and those who least would be prepared to fight court battles over breaches of confidentiality. . . .

The politics of AIDS threatens to create a new national class of "lepers."

Barbara C. Harris, *The Witness*, October 1986.

Regulations governing hospital admissions vary, but, in general, public hospitals are required to treat patients in immediate need of services without questioning their ability to pay. However, hospitals do not necessarily have to admit everyone who walks in, and may go through a review and admission process. There are no clear-cut standards for admission, especially with a relatively new illness like AIDS where possible outcomes are not well known. . . .

People with AIDS have also encountered difficulty in claiming public benefits, such as SSI and SSA, food stamps, or fuel assistance. AIDS has heavily taxed the public benefits system in the large cities with a high incidence of the disease, but the problem extends beyond mere numbers. AIDS strikes a previously healthy and quite young population, while many of the public assistance programs are predicated on covering chronic illnesses or disabilities associated with aging. An estimated 40 to 60 percent of the people with AIDS are un- or underinsured for this type of illness and must seek public assistance to cover their medical care. This creates an additional reason to fear job loss if one's homosexuality or AIDS diagnosis becomes known: the insurance benefits extended by the employer may be the only recourse for a person with AIDS. This is particularly a problem for military personnel, who may be discharged if their homosexuality becomes known. Thus, military men who have AIDS may be extremely reluctant to admit to homosexual behavior or intravenous drug use. . . .

Legal advocates have had to use pressure to get AIDS, and later AIDS-Related Complex (ARC), classified as a disability under SSI, SSA, and other program guidelines. These programs are complicated and difficult to apply for under ordinary circumstances, but in the case of AIDS/ARC, with their wide range of clinical manifestations and unusual age distribution, even entering the system can seem insurmountable. Often, applications are turned down and must be appealed, resulting in lost time and the need for expert assistance. AIDS organizations in the larger cities provide technical assistance by social workers experienced in maneuvering their clients through the maze of welfare programs. In addition, considerable efforts at education and negotiation go on behind the scenes to update the various programs' formulas to be responsive to changing needs.

Intravenous drug users, prostitutes, and Haitians with AIDS face additional problems in obtaining benefits since they live in legal limbo. Some of the affected Haitians are in this country illegally and fear deportation if they make any appearance in a government office. Prostitutes and IV drug users have experienced a history of harassment by these very government agencies and may fear legal reprisal or just plain indifference. Intravenous drug users who are on methadone maintenance programs may also fear jeopardizing their relationship to their clinic if their AIDS diagnosis becomes known when they apply for public assistance. Even more than gay men, at least in urban areas, the IV drug and prostitution subcultures and illegal entrants fear anything that makes them visible to government agencies. . . .

Fear of Disclosure

The Hastings Center is quite right, if dissonant with the new conservatism, in seeing part of the ethical problem in AIDS as a social one: "as a society we must express our moral commitment to the principle that all persons are due a full measure of compassion and respect." Though a bit naive, they rightly see that the people at risk for AIDS will not approach the medical system or its research arms with much trust, and have a well developed interest in less than full compliance. It is not enough for doctors to express the wish to protect their clients or subjects. The doctor or researcher must be prohibited *by law* from releasing names without good reason. And those reasons must be spelled out

Jimmy Margulies, Houston Post, reprinted by permission.

clearly, lest a doctor balance the common good against the individual's rights without full understanding of the social, political, and legal ramifications of doing so. In addition, the researcher must have a reasonable assurance that she/he will not be subjected to government or other harassment, as from insurance companies or employers. Some suggest that medical professionals go a step further in their exhibition of "goodwill": they should publicly support policies, such as civil rights measures, that will improve their subjects' ability to pursue legal remedies and free them from social stigma. Only when lesbians/gay people, Haitians, drug users, and prostitutes no longer fear legal or social reprisal can informed consent, confidentiality, and accurate information be assured.

Some people consider the fear of government subpoena of names and medical information to be sheer paranoia, but both Hastings and Lambda Legal Defense address just that possibility. There is no standard set of case law to deal with the problem of confidentiality, since public health laws are by and large left to each state to administer. But with an increasingly conservative Supreme and District Court judgeship, and the rise of rightist legal theorists who propose far more restrictive constitutional theories, it seems reasonable to imagine the worst possibilities. Hastings suggests that a clear and consistent policy of confidentiality will stand an institution in a better light in court than a less thought-out rationale. But if gay researchers or institutions ultimately refuse to comply with subpoenas, this might as easily be taken as contempt. Lesbian/gay rights are not protected or widely respected enough for individual gay rights to hold up against the ominous "public good."...

There is good reason for paranoia on the part of all the people who have AIDS or who belong to the groups at risk: all are to some degree in violation of law. Homosexuality is illegal in most states; many of the Haitians are illegal entrants to the U.S. and face deportation; and intravenous drug use or ownership of drug injection apparatus is generally illegal. In addition, early in the AIDS epidemic, the Centers for Disease Control several times supplied the names of people with AIDS to other agencies, once by accident. It was clear by the summer of 1983 that the CDC had not taken adequate precautions to insure the confidentiality of those people under its surveillance....

The failure to insure adequate confidentiality measures has many possible consequences. On the most distressing and basic human level, people who need medical treatment may be afraid of going to doctors for fear that their illegal or stigmatized status may become known. While this may vary among those in the major affected groups—gay or bisexual men in the urban gay ghettos, men who have access to gay-sensitive health care and the legal resources of the lesbian/gay community—it is certainly an important factor affecting the decision to seek health care by Haitians and IV drug users.

Concerns of People at Risk

AIDS became a reportable disease in most states by 1983, placing doctors in jeopardy of legal restraint if they failed to report the disease, and bringing at-risk groups more solidly under the surveillance of the Public Health Service and state public health departments. Many public health officials recognized the need to protect clients' confidentiality if they were to get good compliance. They realized that an early concern over the issue of confidentiality would inspire confidence in their protocols and increase the likelihood that healthy but exposed people would voluntarily seek screening or vaccination if they become available. However, government agencies have not been cognizant of the additional concerns of people in risk groups, and have overlooked the past history of abuse of confidentiality and disregard for the special concerns these people have in seeking medical care.

With the increasing right-wing backlash accelerated by AIDS's connection with homosexuality, the penalties for risking exposure as a homosexual increase as a factor in the individual's willingness to seek appropriate medical assistance. The stereotype of gay men as irresponsible and self-destructive has also resulted in the presumption by public health officials that the lesbian/gay community will not cooperate in sex education or voluntarily stop donating blood. Although the medical establishment has in some ways learned that it must cooperate with gay organizations, the bias against considering gay men as cooperative increases in direct proportion to beliefs about their promiscuity. Like the social ideas about sexual behavior, there is a wide, if not always articulated belief, that gay men will not cooperate in attempts to alter their sexual behavior, with no understanding about how the gay male sexual community functions or what messages have been conveyed by the government in the past.

AIDS Encouraging a Pogrom

For several years now, a pogromist spirit directed towards AIDS victims, homosexuals, and even anyone who associates with either of them has been whipped up and fostered in the U.S. The campaign has been played up in the media: demonstrations and school boycotts called by backward and ignorant parents to keep children with AIDS out of schools have been promoted; respectable politicians have fueled stirrings which attack homosexuals in general and which are based on and foster a moral stance of "AIDS is God's punishment for deviance."

Revolutionary Worker, September 22, 1986.

In reality, the lesbian/gay community has launched massive and sensitive educational campaigns about "safe sex," but sex education is so discouraged in this country that several states have considered them insufficient and have begun to make moves toward exercising public health prerogatives to quarantine people with AIDS or establish legal penalties against homosexual acts. California submitted its public health statutes to lawyers, and shortly after that closed all establishments in San Francisco that were believed to have sex on the premises. The bars, baths, and bookstores were allowed to reopen only if they enforced the safe sex guidelines established by a local AIDS organization. Each establishment was required to hire staff to make frequent rounds, and had to insure that a ratio of surveillance staff to clients was maintained.

Deciding To Get Tested

When faced with the choice of improbable but possible exposure to AIDS versus an almost certain harm resulting from admitting to being gay, it is not surprising that a healthy gay man might reasonably decide not to go to the doctor for screening. For bisexual men whose homosexual activity is hidden, or for gay men who live in smaller towns or regions where homosexuality is highly stigmatized or illegal, the equation tips even further against going to a doctor. A paradoxical corollary applies to this concern about the relative harm of coming out versus finding out about AIDS: with the equivocal HTLV-III blood test, openly gay men, who are unaware of the legal or insurance problems a positive test might cause, may rush out to get tested as soon as the test becomes widely available. The lesbian/gay community will experience a widespread and uncontrollable reaction to test results in individuals, as well as possible inter-community tensions which federal agencies may be able to manipulate to their advantage. As AIDS becomes more prevalent outside the urban gay male community, the many different needs of gay men in other living situations may create conditions where legal strategies are undermined by lack of cooperation of gay men who do not understand or are not aware of their civil rights. The great number of false positives from widespread HTLV-III antibody testing may also create a large pool of "straight," low risk people with even more contradictory concerns.

Privacy and civil rights law has tended, under the influence of the new left, feminist, and lesbian/gay movements, to become more inclusive, to extend to categories of people or activities that were not necessarily originally enumerated. As the political climate shifts, however, and the composition of the Supreme Court changes, there is even greater reason to fear that lists originally procured and protected with the best of intentions may later become weapons against disenfranchised groups. The general social concern expressed about AIDS outside the affected groups is not motivated by a desire to help the homosexual, Haitian, IV drug user, or prostitute—as might have been argued in more liberal times, in spite of a tacit moral sentiment against these people— but to protect the "innocent" victims, allegedly including straight men with no risk other than going to prostitutes, from the social deviants who middle Americans believe "produced" AIDS.

Public Good vs. Individual Rights

No one in U.S. society has ever been fully equal under the law, fully innocent until proven guilty, especially when public health is balanced against individual liberties. In the current political climate, . . . there is no pretense that anyone other than traditional, god-fearing, Christian family members deserves equal treatment under the law. The equation promoting the common good is weighted unapologetically against lesbians/gay men, liberated women, third world people, and anything liberal. In a system that says gay men should sacrifice a little freedom to the Public Health Service to produce a greater social good, the lives saved through faithful and well intentioned cooperation with AIDS surveillance and research will not and may not be intended to be those whose lives are at risk.

110

"Clearly, the AIDS epidemic justifies the imposition of legal sanctions to control it."

Civil Rights Are Not as Important as the Public Health

Charles E. Rice

Up to now, the principal victims of AIDS have been homosexual men, who became infected with the virus through anal and oral sex, and intravenous drug users, who spread it by sharing needles. Some people believe that legal sanctions against these acts are the only way to stop the spread of AIDS. In addition, some believe it is necessary to quarantine or otherwise restrict the actions of AIDS carriers. In the following viewpoint, Charles E. Rice, a law professor at Notre Dame University, argues for the enforcement of sodomy laws and other laws either proposed or already in place that he thinks would curtail the spread of the disease.

As you read, consider the following questions:

1. Does the author think homosexual activity is a constitutionally protected right? Supposing that it is, why does he think laws can still be passed that restrict homosexual activity?
2. The author thinks that quarantine measures are necessary to control AIDS. Who would he have quarantined?

Charles E. Rice, "AIDS and the Limits of Law, Parts I and II," *The Wanderer*, March 6 and 13, 1986. Reprinted with permission.

There is still no preventive vaccine and no cure for AIDS. . . . Until a remedy is found, there remains the possibility that it will never be found. Until more is known, public policy should be formulated on the more cautious assumption that no vaccine or cure will be found. Remedial measures ought not to be omitted on the theory that a vaccine or cure is just around the corner.

Sodomy Laws

Clearly, the AIDS epidemic justifies the imposition of legal sanctions to control it. This is so even if homosexual activity is regarded as a constitutionally protected right. Since the enactment of a statute of Henry VIII in 1533, the civil law has punished sodomy as a crime. Theretofore, it was an ecclesiastical offense. Until 1962, all 50 American states had laws punishing homosexual sodomy as a crime.

In 23 states those laws have been repealed by the legislature and in New York and Pennsylvania the highest court of the state has held the sodomy law unconstitutional. Since 1965, the Supreme Court has proclaimed a right of reproductive privacy which the Court found in the "penumbras, formed by emanations from" the Bill of Rights. This right of privacy has been used by the Court to strike down state restrictions on abortion and contraception. While the lower court decisions are in conflict, there is no definitive Supreme Court ruling on the question of whether state prohibitions of sodomy violate this right of privacy, although the Court has summarily upheld, without opinion, state sodomy legislation. . . .

When the highest court of New York held that state's sodomy law unconstitutional in 1981, the court emphasized that "no showing has been made . . . that physical injury is a common or even occasional consequence of the prohibited conduct."

Even within the framework of the Supreme Court's right of privacy, the AIDS epidemic ought to be a sufficient "injury" to justify the prohibition of sodomy. If so, it would seem to follow that lesser restrictions on homosexual activity, including some employment restrictions, could also be upheld. However, the claim that homosexual activity is a preferred constitutional right is strongly urged as a bar to any restriction of that activity. When New York City ordered closed a homosexual bar, the Mine Shaft, which permitted "high-risk sexual activity" to take place on the premises, Thomas B. Stoddard, legislative director of the New York Civil Liberties Union charged that "the governor and the mayor have taken us down a slippery slope that may lead to recriminalization of private sexual conduct in general.". . .

Clearly, statutory restrictions are justified to deal with the AIDS problem. Cong. William E. Dannemeyer (R., Calif.) has introduced five bills in Congress on the subject:

H.R. 3646 provides that no health care facility may receive federal funds if it denies "health care delivery personnel the opportunity to wear protective garments while dealing with patients who have acquired immune deficiency syndrome."

H.R. 3647 provides that no health care facility may receive federal funds if it knowingly permits any "health care delivery personnel who has acquired immune deficiency syndrome to practice in the hospital or facility."

H.R. 3648 would deny federal revenue sharing funds to any "city, town, or other political jurisdiction . . . if it permits the operation of any public bath which is owned or operated by an individual who knows or has reason to know that the bath is hazardous to the public health or who knows or has reason to know it is used for sexual relations between males."

Accept Restrictions To Avoid More Persecution

Fear is the greatest enemy of civil liberties. If we are not to be governed by fear, we have to base our public policy on fact. We have to do this even when the facts hurt some people or deprive them of the enjoyment of their "lifestyles."

In short, if we are going to be able to avoid a nationwide scourging of the homosexuals among us, with all the hatred, anger, finger-pointing, rumormongering, and false accusations such a scourge would entail, we must face the fact that homosexual practices have endangered all of us.

In the scale of national values, civil liberties for homosexuals rank somewhat below survival.

Tom Braden, *Washington Times*, November 7, 1985.

H.R. 3649 would make it a felony, punishable by imprisonment up to 10 years, for any person intentionally to donate blood if "he" knows he "has acquired immune deficiency," "has had sexual relations with a male since 1977," "is an intravenous drug user," or "received a blood transfusion within the past year." This prohibition, according to Cong. Dannemeyer, would apply to "males who have had sex with another male since 1977." It is intended, says Dannemeyer, "to give some teeth to the Centers for Disease Control guidelines which 'suggest' that male homosexuals refrain from donating blood" (*Cong. Rec.*, Oct. 1st, 1985, p. H7986). This bill could be more precisely worded to clarify which if any of its categories apply to female as well as male donors.

H. Cong. Res. 224 would express the sense of Congress that public schools should not permit students with AIDS or AIDS-related complex to attend classes and should make alternative arrangements for such students to receive education.

The Dannemeyer proposals are sensible and limited and they should be enacted. A variety of other measures has already been implemented or proposed by state and federal authorities. The Texas health department has proposed a rule to quarantine "incorrigible" AIDS patients who refuse to curtail sexual activities that could spread the disease. The rule was proposed after a male homosexual who had AIDS refused to stop working as a Houston prostitute. He later died. No other state has such a quarantine law. The proposal has been criticized on the ground that it could drive homosexuals underground and thus make it more difficult to control the disease.

The San Antonio City Health Department has formally warned 14 AIDS patients to refrain from sexual activity and to avoid sharing needles or donating blood or plasma and has required them to warn physicians and dentists with whom they come into contact. The order was issued under the authority of the Texas Communicable Disease Prevention and Control Act, which allows controls on people who are health risks to the community. Jeffrey Levi, political director of the National Gay Task Force, charged that the action would "stigmatize all people with AIDS and suggest that they would behave irresponsibly when there's no evidence that 99.9 percent of them are not behaving responsibly."

Health Regulations

Various agencies have adopted guidelines to deal with possible risks arising from the lack of certainty as to the way that AIDS is transmitted. In August, 1985, after the discovery of the AIDS virus in the tears of one patient, the Centers for Disease Control issued guidelines for the protection of health workers coming into contact with tears, including those who fit contact lenses.

The Indiana State Board of Health's Division of Dental Health has advised dentists to "wear gloves, masks, protective eyewear, and protective gowns to keep them from coming into contact with blood seepage that often accompanies dental procedures."

The CDC has proposed that women at high risk for the AIDS virus should be tested for it and counseled so as to avoid transmission of AIDS to infants. Presumably, such counseling could include encouragement of abortion.

The U.S Public Health Service has declared that the safety rules for hepatitis cases are sufficient for use with respect to AIDS. Dr. James O. Mason, acting assistant secretary of Health and Human Services, declared that since AIDS is not spread by casual contact, the service does not recommend routine AIDS antibody screening for workers in occupations where there is no known risk of AIDS virus transmission. Dr. Mason described as "totally unfounded" the fear that the AIDS virus might be transmitted in food handled by infected workers. "Food service workers known to be infected with AIDS should not be restricted from work unless they have another infection or illness for which such restriction would be warranted," the PHS guidelines declared.

In January, 1986, it was disclosed that the PHS had drafted guidelines urging surgeons, dentists, and obstetricians to take special precautions against the transmission of the AIDS virus. The draft guidelines state that "in the dental setting, as in the operative and obstetric setting, gloves should be changed between all patient contacts."

By Clyde Wells, The Augusta Chronicle. © by and permission of North America Syndicate, 1987.

The guidelines do not recommend routine testing of prison inmates for the AIDS virus; the guidelines note that such testing would not be feasible unless the prison were prepared to provide separate facilities for those who test positive. There have been 455 confirmed cases of AIDS among inmates in 25 state and federal correctional systems and 310 cases in the jails of 19 cities or countries.

The American College Health Association, however, has declared that there is "no reason to exclude AIDS victims or carriers from campus academic, social, or cultural activities" and "no medical reason whatever to alter dormitory assignments simply because of a gay or bisexual roommate."

The military services have instituted measures to separate carriers of the AIDS virus, as well as active homosexuals, from the service. As a general rule there is no doctor-patient privilege of confidentiality in the military, and the incompatibility of AIDS with the performance of the military mission would seem to justify such separation no matter how the condition was discovered.

The federal Health and Human Services Department has drafted a regulation to deny immigration to foreigners with AIDS.

Registering AIDS Carriers

One important issue is whether to require a registry of AIDS victims and of AIDS virus carriers. This has been proposed in several states. Dr. James W. Curran, chief of AIDS research at CDC, has said that the entire population of the United States may need vaccination against AIDS if a vaccine is developed. Dr. Curran wants to create a "donor referral registry," listing those who test positive for antibodies to the AIDS virus, so as to protect the nation's blood supply.

British magistrates have power to order a person to be taken to a hospital and kept there if the local authorities consider him an AIDS risk to others. The local authorities may also prevent relatives of a person who has died of AIDS from taking possession of the body. The British authorities are required to take "all reasonably practical steps" to prevent people coming near or into contact with the body of a person who has died of AIDS. The National Public Safety Board of Sweden has recommended maximum two-year prison sentences for AIDS patients who have sexual relations with persons who do not have AIDS.

Meanwhile, the Los Angeles City Council has approved an ordinance barring discrimination against AIDS patients in jobs, housing, and health care.

If the experts are right and AIDS cannot be spread by casual contact, legal restrictions against high-risk categories could possibly suffice to deal with the problem. The ultimate measure of quarantine could be appropriate with respect to AIDS patients, active homosexuals, intravenous drug users, and prostitutes. However, the number of such persons who would have to be quarantined could be very large. If AIDS maintains its present rate of growth, which is unlikely, the entire population of the United States will have AIDS within 20 years. If quarantine or lesser restrictions against high-risk categories are to be effective, they will have to be imposed fairly quickly.

The Common Good

To those afflicted with AIDS, all possible help should be given in accord with the Christian injunction that it is just as important to love the sinner as it is to hate the sin. The action of Mother Teresa and her nuns and of other religious groups of various denominations in providing shelter and care to AIDS victims provides an example.

A Christian response, however, requires also the protection of the common good. The first step in that protection is for the law to affirm the objective wrongness of the degraded behavior that has led to the problem. To the claim that there is any legal or moral right to practice the vices which have generated the disease, the only coherent response a civilized society can make is total prohibition. Congress, the state legislatures, and the courts should repudiate the false notion that homosexual practice is a constitutional right. Sodomy laws should be enforced. Those who practice that vice have no right to claim that it be excluded from consideration in determining their eligibility for positions of responsibility, including teaching and government service.

AIDS Is a Health, Not a Civil Rights, Issue

Paradoxically, the truly humanitarian position in the face of an AIDS plague is that we not identify with the victims and instead cast our lot with what in earlier times was dubbed the "common good." . . .

This argument is not a counsel against good medical care or proper concern for AIDS victims. Nor is it a suggestion that we curtail any "right" that doesn't potentially imperil the lives of others.

This is not a civil-rights issue; this is a medical issue. Yet social and legal solutions to the AIDS problem are proceeding at a pace disproportionate to the knowledge that experts now possess concerning the illness.

Richard Restak, *Los Angeles Times*, September 13, 1985.

This is not to suggest discrimination for its own sake. But a balance has to be restored in the law, consistent with the reality that homosexual activity is a social as well as a moral evil. Similarly, the role of intravenous drug abuse in the spread of AIDS requires intensified enforcement of the law against the drug trade. . . .

Even if AIDS is not spread by casual contact, no remedial program will be effective without a national redirection of sexual ethics. . . .

Authentically Insane

Finally, the legitimization of homosexual activity is predictable in a contraceptive society, which cannot say that homosexual relations are objectively wrong without condemning itself. Instead, homosexual living must be regarded as an "alternate lifestyle"— which it is if sex has no inherent relation to reproduction. If it is entirely a matter of individual option whether sex will be used for recreational or procreational purposes, there is no intrinsic reason why Freddy cannot marry George. The objections to homosexual marriage are reduced to the esthetic and pragmatic. Of course, a society with no basis in principle for deciding whether boys should marry girls or other boys is not only on the road to extinction, it is authentically insane.

AIDS "will end the sexual revolution," says Dr. Donald Francis of CDC. "You can take your chances with herpes or hepatitis B, but you can't take your chances with this." A sound response to the AIDS epidemic, however, requires a national examination of conscience, a rejection of the contraceptive ethic in all its manifestations, a national purpose of amendment to return to the full observance of the law of God and, indispensably, a commitment to prayer and repentance.

In human terms there is a possibility that we are done for, that we are exterminating ourselves by our self-indulgence. Even if a vaccine or cure for AIDS is found, it may provide only a reprieve since it is predictable that new diseases will arise if we continue on our "liberated" course, as chlamydia, now epidemic, was unknown until recently. If we seek a solution only through science and the law, our efforts will fail. It is time instead that we took Christ at His word: "Without me you can do nothing" (*John* 15:6). And it is time we turned from the politicians, lawyers, doctors, and sexologists and resorted instead to the intercession of the Mother of God who is the patroness of this nation.

"The disabling effects of the disease on its victims qualify as handicaps but . . . the ability of the victims to spread the disease . . . is not a handicap."

AIDS Carriers Can Be Discriminated Against in the Workplace

Charles J. Cooper

Can an employer fire or refuse to hire a person who has the AIDS virus? In the following viewpoint, Charles J. Cooper, Assistant Attorney General with the United States Justice Department, argues that the Federal Rehabilitation Act, which protects the handicapped from discrimination, does not apply to carriers of the AIDS virus. Having an infectious disease is not considered a handicap under the law, he believes. If they fear contagion, employers have a right to fire or refuse to hire AIDS carriers.

As you read, consider the following questions:

1. Why does Cooper believe that having an infectious disease is not in itself a handicap under the law?
2. According to Cooper, does an employer need to explain or defend his or her fear of contagion? Why or why not?
3. Why, according to the author, are employees with AIDS a legitimate concern for employers?

Charles J. Cooper, "Applications of Section 504 of the Rehabilitation Act to Persons with AIDS, AIDS-Related Complex, or Infection with the AIDS Virus," Office of Legal Counsel, U.S. Department of Justice, June 20, 1986.

119

We have concluded that section 504 [of the Discrimination Act of 1973] prohibits discrimination based on the disabling effects that AIDS and related conditions may have on their victims. By contrast, we have concluded that an individual's (real or perceived) ability to transmit the disease to others is not a handicap within the meaning of the statute and, therefore, that discrimination on this basis does not fall within section 504. . . .

Statute Language

Section 504 of the Rehabilitation Act of 1973 generally proscribes discrimination against the handicapped in programs or activities that are conducted by federal agencies or that receive federal funds. In relevant part, the statute provides:

> No otherwise qualified handicapped individual in the United States, shall, solely by reason of his handicap, be excluded from the participation in, be denied the benefits of, or be subjected to discrimination under any program or activity receiving Federal financial assistance or under any program or activity conducted by any Executive agency or by the United States Postal Service. . . .

In applying section 504 to the problems addressed in this opinion, the initial question is whether [carriers of the AIDS virus] are "handicapped" within the meaning of section 504. The Rehabilitation Act provides that a person is handicapped if he

> (i) has a physical or mental impairment which substantially limits one or more of such person's major life activities, (ii) has a record of such an impairment, or (iii) is regarded as having such an impairment.

Applying this definition to persons suffering from AIDS, we have little difficulty concluding that the disabling effects of the disease on its victims qualify as handicaps. . . .

Although AIDS victims are handicapped in the ways noted above, it does not necessarily follow that every aspect of the disease constitutes a handicap within the meaning of the statute. . . .

We therefore turn to the question of whether the ability to transmit a disease is by itself enough to render the carrier handicapped within the meaning of the statute. In examining this question, it is helpful to hypothesize the case of a carrier who is personally immune to the disease. This hypothetical isolates as purely as possible the communicable feature of the disease from any adverse effects it may ordinarily have on a host.

An "Immune Carrier"

It is clear to us that an immune carrier does not fall within the statutory definition of a person handicapped in fact—*i.e.*, one who "has a physical or mental impairment which substantially limits one or more of such person's major life activities." An immune

"THE SUPREME COURT SAYS I STILL GET TO WORK HERE EVEN IF I DO CARRY AIDS!... DON'T I GET A VICTORY KISS?!..."

By Bob Gorrell, The Richmond News Leader. © by and permission of North America Syndicate, 1987.

carrier does not have "a physical or mental impairment," because the carrier's condition—the presence within his body of the active infectious agent—has no adverse physical consequences for him. . . .

Second, even if the carrier has an "impairment," it does not substantially limit any major life activity. The carrier is fully capable of performing all major life activities, including those listed in the HHS regulations—*i.e.*, "caring for [him]self, performing manual tasks, walking, seeing, hearing, speaking, breathing, learning, and working." The carrier may be analogized to a perfectly healthy person carrying a test tube containing the infectious agent. This person may possess the ability to spread the disease to others, but there is no basis for arguing that he is handicapped.

To be sure, a carrier of a contagious disease may suffer adverse social and professional consequences. Persons susceptible to the disease may be reluctant to associate with him, but a person cannot be regarded as handicapped simply because others shun his company. Otherwise, a host of personal traits—from ill-temper to poor personal hygiene—would constitute handicaps, a conclusion which the drafters of the regulations recognized to be untenable.

In light of our conclusion that an immune carrier cannot qualify as handicapped on the ground that he has an impairment that substantially limits his major life activities, it follows that he cannot qualify on the ground that he "has a record of such an impairment" or "is regarded as having such an impairment." Since the ability to transmit a disease is not an impairment, the fact that an individual was able to transmit the disease in the past (or was misclassified as having had such an ability) does not mean that he has "a record of . . . an impairment." Likewise, the perception that the individual is able to spread the disease does not mean that he "is regarded as having . . . an impairment," for the perceived condition, even if actual, is not an impairment within the meaning of the statute.

In sum, it seems clear that a person who carries but is personally immune to a communicable disease cannot on that basis qualify as handicapped under section 504. . . . The mere fact that he is, was, or is thought to be able to communicate a debilitating disease, standing alone, is not enough.

Contagiousness Not a Handicap

If, as we have concluded, the ability of an immune carrier to spread a contagious disease is not itself a handicap, there is no basis for reaching a different conclusion with respect to communicability when the person carrying the disease is not immune and in fact suffers from its disabling effects. Communicability alone is not a handicap in the former situation, and it does not become a handicap in the latter simply because it is accompanied by the disease's disabling effects. Accordingly, we conclude with respect to AIDS sufferers (a) that the disabling effects of the disease on its victims qualify as handicaps but (b) that the ability of the victims to spread the disease to others is not a handicap. . . .

A person who is discriminated against because he is (or is regarded as) seropositive has no claim under section 504. Nor can he challenge the reasonableness of the defendant's judgement about the risk that he will spread the disease; defendants are not prohibited by section 504 from making incorrect, and even irrational, decisions so long as their decisions are not based on handicap. . . .

Concern Need Not Be Reasonable

It should be noted that the reasonableness of an employer's concern about the spread of disease is relevant only to the extent it bears on the question of pretext. As we have shown, section 504 simply does not reach decisions based on fear of contagion— whether reasonable or not—so long as it is not in truth a pretext for discrimination on account of handicap. An employer, for example, who makes hiring decisions based on an unreasonable concern about contagion is no different from an employer whose hiring decisions rest on any other unreasonable basis that lies outside section 504's limited reach. . . .

Whatever the medical facts regarding transmissibility might be, a constellation of factors make it intuitively plausible that a person claiming fear of contagion genuinely discriminated on that basis rather than by reason of handicap. The consequences of contracting the virus are severe; there is a substantial chance, possibly even approaching 100%, that the infected individual will eventually contract the disease. And the disease itself is both incurable and fatal—it appears that everyone who contracts it will die. In common experience, even a very low probability of contracting a contagious virus with consequences of this magnitude is likely to call forth a strongly-felt response. In addition, there are a number of questions regarding AIDS on which the medical community does not speak with one voice. Knowledge of the disease is growing and, in some respects, changing rapidly. The mechanisms of transmission are still not fully understood, and epidemiological evidence does not permit the kind of categorical statements about risk that would make one doubt the legitimacy of claims of fear. . . .

Conclusion

For the foregoing reasons, we conclude that discrimination based on the disabling effects of AIDS on its victims may violate section 504, but that the statute does not restrict measures taken to prevent the spread of the disease.

"The problem of AIDS in the workplace is not contagion. It is . . . fear itself."

AIDS Carriers Should Not Be Discriminated Against in the Workplace

Charles Krauthammer

In the following viewpoint, Charles Krauthammer argues that fear of contagion of AIDS in the workplace is irrational. He further states that the Federal Rehabilitation Act, which protects the handicapped person from discrimination, also protects the AIDS victim. Krauthammer is a syndicated columnist and a senior editor of *The New Republic*.

As you read, consider the following questions:

1. Krauthammer makes an analogy between the Cooper memorandum on AIDS and a court opinion concerning fear of the working nuclear reactor at Three Mile Island. What is his point? Do you agree or disagree?
2. Why does Krauthammer think that Charles Cooper's interpretation of the Rehabilitation Act is actually going against the purpose of the Act?

Charles Krauthammer, "Ignorance Is Cause but Not Justification for AIDS Bias," *Los Angeles Times*, June 30, 1986. © 1986, Washington Post Writers Group, reprinted with permission.

Two years after the accident at Unit 2 nuclear reactor at Three Mile Island, a court suit was filed to prevent the restarting of the other, undamaged, reactor. The argument was not that this reactor was a health hazard. The Nuclear Regulatory Commission had produced 22,000 pages of hearing transcripts to determine that it was not.

The argument instead was that people believed that it was dangerous. Thus if TMI 1 were reopened it might produce "intense anxiety" (tension and fear, accompanied by physical disorders including skin rashes, aggravated ulcers, and skeletal and muscular problems), and that would be a hazard to the surrounding communities.

A novel idea. Something is safe, but because people think it is dangerous that makes it, well, (psychologically) unsafe. Perception is reality. The U.S. Supreme Court, however, was unimpressed with this novelty. It ruled, unanimously, that the commission did not have to consider imaginary effects.

Fear Is Not Enough

Fear is undoubtedly an unpleasant state, but in itself does not create actionable claims. If it did, the line of litigants invoking such claims would be endless. Is there anything, after all, that people do not irrationally fear? If a groundless fear is enough to endow one with legal rights, then there is no piece of nonsense that cannot result in yet another claim on others. Your neighbor has a dog. The dog is harmless. But you are afraid of dogs anyway. Can you impound the dog?

In the case of Three Mile Island, the Reagan Justice Department argued no. Now, another year, another place and another piece of nonsense. The hysteria this time is not about gamma rays but about AIDS, the irradiated irrationality of the 1980s.

Discrimination Laws Debased

The Justice Department has considered again the question of whether perception is reality. It issued a ruling on what kind of discrimination is permissible against AIDS victims. The Rehabilitation Act of 1973 prohibits discrimination on the basis of handicap. The Justice Department decided that an employer may not fire an AIDS victim if the employer is concerned about the "disabling effect of AIDS." But he may fire the victims if he is concerned about the contagious effects of AIDS.

Of course, in the workplace there are no contagious effects. You have about as much chance of catching AIDS in the workplace as you do of catching cancer or multiple sclerosis. So: Your employee has AIDS or cancer or MS. The employee is harmless. But you are afraid of him anyway. Can you fire him? Says the Justice Department, yes.

125

The immediate effect of this ruling will be to permit AIDS firings left and right. Is there an easier claim than the claim of irrational fear? The more general effect is to debase the idea underlying the anti-discrimination laws. The whole point of such laws is to say this: It may indeed cause you psychological distress to mix with others whom you irrationally dislike or fear. Too bad. The state has decided that these particular prejudices are destructive and irrational. Therefore the state will prohibit you—even in "private-sector" transactions such as hiring or firing or serving people in your own luncheonette—from acting upon your groundless prejudices.

The point of the Rehabilitation Act was to add another class of irrationality—irrationality about the disabled—to the catalogue of those that the state will no longer countenance. Now comes the Justice Department, in essence, to add: "—except for one category of irrationality, fear of contagion. The state will permit you to fire disabled people on that account."

Not Much Hope for Rights

The Centers for Disease Control and the Public Health Service, as well as private physicians in every major locality affected by AIDS, agree that the syndrome cannot be transmitted by casual contact and that it is, in fact, less communicable than many viral and sexually transmitted diseases. Some courts have ruled that children with AIDS, a growing category of victims, cannot be barred from school. But the Justice Department says that the fear of catching the disease is enough to sanction discrimination unless that fear is merely "a pretext for discrimination on account of handicap." Furthermore, a positive antibody test result may be a legitimate ground for discrimination. The person with AIDS, or the one who is seropositive for the virus, must prove that he or she is not contagious and that the discriminatory act was motivated purely by prejudice due to the disability. Patients would then have to pursue their rights through the Reagan court system, not an optimistic prospect.

The Nation, July 5/12, 1986.

Even as a piece of reasoning this casuistry fails. After all, why in general do people shrink from (and end up discriminating against) disability if not from fear of contagion? Moreover, if contagion were really the problem, private employers would not have to worry about it at all. The state can handle that. It has more sweeping powers against people with serious contagious diseases than it does against criminals. If you are innocent of all sin but have tuberculosis, the government can lock you away.

The problem of AIDS in the workplace is not contagion. It is, as someone well acquainted with disability once said, fear itself. Fear itself does not deserve special protection in our public life.

There is no greater intellectual laziness than the proposition that perception is reality. The last place that Orwellian slogan ought to find refuge is in the law. The whole point of the law is to determine which perceptions are real and which aren't, and to give legal standing to one and not the other.

It does not matter if people think you murdered. If you didn't you don't go to jail. It does not matter if people think TMI 1 is dangerous. If it isn't, it stays open. It should not matter if people think that you can get AIDS in the Xerox room. You can't. Ignorance is a cause of discrimination. It is not a justification for it.

> *"Stiffer legislative penalties must be imposed on those who endanger the lives of others."*

Legal Restrictions Are Needed To Control AIDS

Gene Antonio

The law can be used effectively to control the behavior of AIDS carriers, according to Gene Antonio, a free lance investigative journalist and social commentator. In the following viewpoint, he lists a series of legal measures he believes the Federal government should enact to control the spread of AIDS.

As you read, consider the following questions:

1. How does Antonio respond to the argument that the government can't legislate morality?
2. Why does the author think having too many legal restrictions on people's behavior is better than not having enough?
3. Why does Antonio believe that the government should authorize employers and insurers to screen out potential AIDS carriers in choosing employees or policy holders?

The AIDS Cover-Up? by Gene Antonio, published in 1986 by Ignatius Press, 15 Oakland Avenue, Harrison, NY 10528. Reprinted with permission.

The prohomosexual political chauvinism which prevails in many municipalities and states has gravely impaired the credibility of local officials in dealing objectively with the AIDS epidemic. High risk carriers of AIDS are being systematically protected and the lives of countless others put in jeopardy by the unwillingness and inability of state and local officials to take effective action to stop its spread.

Federal action is essential if the "Typhoid Mikes and Marys" of the AIDS epidemic are to be prevented from continuing to infect others individually and en masse.

Legislating Morality

Any suggestion that legal measures should be ultilized to combat the AIDS crisis has been met with the objection of ostensible civil libertarians that it is impossible to legislate morality. This contention involves sophistry. All legislation is inextricably interwoven with some underlying system of ethics. Laws against murder and stealing are based on the Mosaic law. Laws against drunk driving are based on the narrow moral view asserting that the right of the general citizenry to live supersedes the "right" of the individual to drive recklessly. . . .

In a sense, it is correct that you cannot legislate an individual's sense of enjoyment in abiding by the law. The potential drunk driver, rapist or thug may never like the fact that his personal preferences are being curtailed by legislative mandate. There will always be those who choose to violate the law and risk the penalties involved.

Nevertheless, legal sanctions do foster a general external obedience, even among those unwillingly inclined. Only an anarchist would contend that because we have individuals who murder, rape, steal and drive while drunk that we should abolish all laws prohibiting such antisocial behavior. If anything, many today would argue that stiffer legislative penalties must be imposed on those who endanger the lives of others.

Likewise, there will always be those who choose to engage in behavior putting themselves and others at risk of AIDS infection. A lack of personal self-preservation and moral responsibility notwithstanding, legal restrictions can significantly curtail the number of opportunities available for these individuals to acquire and disseminate AIDS infection. The so-called "right to privacy" is abrogated when acts done in private result in the spread of a deadly public epidemic. . . .

Legislative Steps To Halt AIDS Spread

1. *Empower and support the Surgeon General to take practical measures to halt the spread of AIDS.*

Fortunately, there is federal legislation on the books right now which could significantly hinder the unrestricted spread of AIDS contagion by those knowingly spreading the disease. The Federal Code states:

264. *Control of communicable diseases*

(a) The Surgeon General, with the approval of the Administrator [Secretary], is authorized to make and enforce such regulations as in his judgment are necessary to prevent the introduction, transmission, or spread of communicable diseases from foreign countries into the States or possessions, or from one State or possession into any other State or possession. . . .

(b) On recommendation of the National Advisory Health Council, regulations prescribed under this section may provide for the apprehension and examination of any individual reasonably believed to be infected with a communicable disease in a communicable stage and (1) to be moving or about to move from a State to another State; or (2) to be a probable source of infection to individuals who, while infected with such disease in a communicable stage, will be moving from a State to another State. Such regulations may provide that if upon examination any such individual is found to be infected, he may be detained for such time and in such manner as may be reasonable and necessary. *United States Code Service*, 42 USCS, The Public Health and Welfare.

Paying for Our Permissiveness

We know how the disease is spread and do little to discourage it.

Just the opposite has been happening. It has been proven that AIDS is spread mainly by the dirty needles of drug users and the activities of homosexuals and bisexuals. Yet the sexual deviates have been encouraged and the drug users treated permissively. . . .

It is insanity at the same time to refuse to look at the ways in which AIDS is spread. In the past, when it was shown that rats spread bubonic plague, the effort to control the disease included controlling the rats. When mosquitoes were discovered to spread malaria, they were controlled as well. . . .

We . . . think society better face the facts and recognize that it is reaping the bitter harvest of its permissiveness.

Nackey Loeb, *Union Leader*, June 25, 1986.

Infectious tuberculosis is already included under this provision. The signing of an executive order by the President naming the disease at risk is all that is required for the Surgeon General to put the above provisions in effect regarding those who would intentionally put others in danger of acquiring AIDS. . . .

2. *Federal order closing down all known homosexual bathhouses.* . . .

Passing out condoms, erecting billboards and handing out flyers suggesting that bathhouse patrons "play safely" are missing the point. If you have a dining establishment whose patrons are continually dying of food poisoning, you don't hand out stomach pumps to customers going in—you close the restaurant.

As a first practical step to stemming the most blatant, teeming sources of AIDS contagion, the high-risk homosexual bathhouses and "clubs" must be closed permanently by federal edict.

3. *Federal bans on all high-risk group members from:*
—*donating blood or plasma.*
—*contributing semen to sperm banks.*
—*donating organs.*

The present AIDS blood screening test still permits a certain percentage of those infected with AIDS to slip through the safety net and endanger people's lives. All prospective donors of any of these protected substances must be required to sign a statement under oath that they are not members of a high-risk group. Mandatory high federal penalties would be imposed on violators.

Necessity of Proper Precautions

4. *Hospital officials must allow medical personnel to take proper precautions when dealing with AIDS patients. Proper precautions must be taken to protect non-AIDS patients from those with AIDS.*

Some hospital administrations are not permitting personnel to take necessary safety precautions (mask, gown, goggles) in dealing with AIDS patients (so as to avoid "stigmatizing"). Pregnant nurses are not being informed that they are dealing with AIDS patients despite the grave risk to their unborn child. In some hospitals, AIDS patients are being put in the same ward or room with immunocompromised non-AIDS patients. This is a violation of the non-AIDS patient's right to safe care and right to know. Staff and personnel desiring to take precautions for themselves or to inform the non-AIDS patients at risk are threatened with dismissal. These and other practices threatening the lives of noninfected personnel and patients must cease.

5. *Federal registration of all persons diagnosed with full-blown AIDS, pre-AIDS (ARC) and those testing positive with the AIDS blood screening test.*

Contact tracing for prior and present sexual contacts must be implemented.

Persons with serious AIDS virus-induced disease without CDC-defined AIDS or immunosuppression (e.g., AIDS virus-induced dementia and tuberculosis) must be considered included under this definition. . . .

Pre-AIDS or ARC patients must be reported. Persons who are shown to be asymptomatically infected must be reported. If any practical efforts are to be made to halt the spread of AIDS infection, it is essential to find out who is infected and take practical steps to prevent these persons from infecting others.

From the standpoint of those who have been unknowingly infected with AIDS, it is essential that they be informed that: 1. they are at risk for developing the disease, and 2. they must take steps to avoid spreading the disease to others.

With a view toward preserving public health, it is absolutely crucial to track down those who may be unknowingly or knowingly disseminating the AIDS virus. To make no efforts whatsoever to determine who is infected is to encourage further rapid AIDS spread.

Federal penalties would be imposed on physicians failing to report persons diagnosed with full-blown AIDS, intermediate AIDS or the asymptomatically infected.

6. *There must be a federal crackdown on pornography soliciting persons for high-risk sexual activities. Computerized solicitation for high-risk sexual activities and the efforts of paedophiles to seek children must be stopped. . . .*

Test All To Control AIDS

Universal testing, . . . provided that it were regular, would successfully identify all—or nearly all—carriers. Some actual or potential carriers, particularly among the high-risk groups, might be driven "underground" by fear of being identified and isolated: but the risk to the population from these few would be considerably smaller than the present risk from those who are spreading the disease because they are not known to be carriers. Regular testing would greatly curtail the damage done by those carriers who remained at large.

Christopher Monckton, *The American Spectator*, January 1987.

---

7. *There must be a crackdown on massage parlors and vice rings promoting anonymous heterosexual promiscuity.*

AIDS spread is also fostered through establishments promoting and commercially exploiting anonymous heterosexual promiscuity. A significant number of female prostitutes have already become infected with the AIDS virus through drug abuse and bisexual males. Prostitution appears to be a major source of AIDS transmission in Africa and is a major danger for AIDS spread in the United States.

8. *Federal authorization for public and private employers to utilize AIDS risk factor questionnaires and AIDS blood screening tests in hiring. Insurance companies must be permitted to utilize these means in selecting applicants.*

Although nonsexual, nonblood transfusion-related AIDS transmission has been discounted by the CDC, other medical authorities have indicated other routes as viable means of AIDS transmission. AIDS is a lentivirus. Its incubation period is deceptively lengthy and its modes of transmission not fully understood. The genetic variability of the AIDS virus can produce dangerous changes in modes of transmission.

Researchers have already found out that AIDS is more deadly than was previously anticipated. Since AIDS is a terminal disease, it is far better to err on the side of caution now than tragically to realize later on that its capacity for spread was more potent than first contended.

Employers must have the option of refusing to hire AIDS carriers so as to protect others in the workplace. Dr. Slaff reports that General Reassurance Corporation has found the amount on all AIDS life insurance claims typically five times the average. Some states have laws prohibiting discrimination of any kind based on AIDS virus infection. Insurance companies must be able to screen out AIDS-infected individuals so as to guard against the enormous losses such as those they have already sustained in AIDS claims.

Some states and municipalities have laws prohibiting the questioning of a prospective employee regarding his sexual behavior or orientation. These must be overridden in the interests of public safety.

Positive Sex Education

9. *Sex education in the public schools must include instruction in sound healthful principles of sexual interaction.*

A concerted effort must be made to prevent the AIDS epidemic from gaining a foothold in the nation's elementary, junior high and secondary schools. . . .

Teenagers and children need to be instructed to refrain from sexual intercourse outside of marriage. They must be taught the grievous medical, personal and social consequences of heterosexual promiscuity.

Homosexuality per se must be taught as an unhealthy, unsafe and lethal sexual alternative. "It's a very major risk to enter these communities," warns June Osborn, Dean of Public Health at the University of Michigan and a professor of epidemiology. "So the fifteen or sixteen-year-old kid who's going to declare his same-sex preference should understand that there's a serious chance of infection that can truly be a matter of life and death."

The shock waves of the AIDS epidemic are just beginning to be felt outside the homosexual subculture. Soon, very soon, the devastating social and economic repercussions of the epidemic will be seen and felt among all segments of society. The entire population will shudder as the anguished cries of the demented and dying rise in a ghastly crescendo. Unless drastic measures are taken to prevent the epidemic from spreading, AIDS may well become *everyone's* Final Epidemic.

"Isolation would needlessly confine many individuals who are nondangerous."

Legal Restrictions Won't Control AIDS

Larry Gostin and William J. Curran

Public health officials have been reluctant to impose mandatory blood testing to find AIDS carriers or to use isolation to control the spread of the disease. In the following viewpoint, Larry Gostin and William J. Curran, faculty members of the Harvard University School of Public Health, state that the marginal benefits of imposing legal restrictions on AIDS carriers are not worth the damage done to voluntary efforts to control the disease.

As you read, consider the following questions:

1. What problems do the authors believe must be addressed before voluntary contact of sexual partners by AIDS carriers can be effective?
2. Why, according to Gostin and Curran, would mandatory tracing of the sexual partners of AIDS carriers by public health officials be less effective in controlling AIDS than it has been in controlling syphilis?
3. What reasons do the authors give to show that general isolation of AIDS carriers is impractical?
4. Why would it be difficult to prove criminal intent on the part of someone who has given the AIDS virus to someone else?

Larry Gostin and William J. Curran, "The Limits of Compulsion in Controlling AIDS," *The Hastings Center Report*, December 1986. Reproduced by permission. © The Hastings Center.

AIDS poses an unparalleled challenge for health policy makers seeking methods to reduce its spread and to help ensure public safety, consistent with the protection of individual rights. Pressure is mounting on public health officials to consider compulsory infection control strategies. Many see the use of compulsion as necessary to counter the epidemic. . . .

The classic public health response to communicable disease, developed in the late nineteenth and early twentieth centuries, is to identify those who harbor the virus by casefinding (testing and screening); to report infectious individuals to public health officials, who keep a register; and to treat or to modify the behavior of those capable of transmitting the infection. . . .

We will examine control measures that directly impinge on individual liberty, including sexual contact tracing, [isolation], and the use of the criminal law.

Voluntary Notification

Programs of contact notification can occur on two levels: voluntary notification by the client or statutory notification by the public health department. The U.S. Centers for Disease Control (CDC) has recommended the first level of notification by the client in recent guidelines to reduce the transmission of HIV infection. The CDC recommends that serologic testing to detect the presence of antibodies to HIV should be routinely offered to all persons at increased risk of contracting HIV infection. Infected persons should then be counseled to "inform previous sexual partners and any persons with whom needles were shared of their potential exposure to HIV and encourage them to seek counseling/testing." This first level of contact notification is the least intrusive, for it takes place within the confidential health care professional/client relationship, and relies upon the client's voluntary cooperation.

Notification of sexual partners by seropositive individuals can be beneficial, since its objective is to inform the partners that they have been exposed to the infection. The notification provides an opportunity to seek further diagnostic information, including serologic testing; to be counseled; and to modify reproductive, sexual, or drug-using behavior.

CDC guidelines, however, do not address a number of troubling matters: (1) there have been few studies designed to answer the critical question of whether knowledge of sero-status actually influences behavior and, if so, in what direction; (2) there are insufficient resources and services to ensure that testing, public health information, and counseling are provided in a reliable and professional manner; and (3) there are insufficient statutory protections of confidentiality for the client and his or her contacts.

The second level of notification of contacts is more properly termed contact tracing, a form of medical surveillance in which public health officials seek to discover the sexual partners of . . . (a known infected person) and then seek to prevent further spread of the disease, if possible, by treating those contacts. Contact tracing is specifically authorized in many venereal disease statutes across the country. The health care professional reports his or her client's name to the health department; the name is entered on a register; and the public health officer then has a statutory power or duty to inquire about the person's previous and current sexual partners. . . .

Once a sexual contact has been located, public health officers generally do have statutory power to order a physical examination and treatment. Public health officials must, however, have reasonable grounds for believing that the contact is infected and is refusing treatment. . . .

Quarantine Will Run Disease Underground

Quarantine in this department has been opposed from the outset. What does it accomplish, really? We do not know the period during which this disease is infectious. And that's important.

If we are quarantining people, we need to know when this disease becomes infectious. Otherwise it cannot be an effective tool. I think it will do more to run the disease underground. If there is an understanding that we will quarantine people, physicians will not report to us. And we will not know what the trend is, how many cases, etc. If we run it underground, you'll never know the dimensions of the problem, you'll never know how to allocate resources. We do not want to put into place any measures that will prevent or discourage physicians from reporting cases of AIDS.

Bailus Walker, Massachusetts Commissioner of Public Health, interviewed in *Gay Community News*, December 7, 1985.

There are strong reasons against statutory contact tracing as a public health response to the AIDS epidemic. First, the direct public health benefits would be marginal; and, second, the introduction of intrusive measures would seriously undermine other existing public health efforts to contain the spread of the disease.

Limits of Contacting

From a public health perspective, the major question is what use would be made of the data collected from a program of sexual contact tracing. Investigation of sexual partners is most effective when there is a preventive vaccine or therapy. There is an undisputed public health benefit of locating persons potentially exposed to an infectious agent when an effective medical intervention is possible. The availability of penicillin to treat gonorrhea or syphilis, for example, not only preserves the health of the infected person, but also prevents that person from transmitting the disease unless he or she becomes reinfected. Because no such medical intervention exists in relation to AIDS, use of the data would be restricted to education and counseling; public health educational programs and counseling should be available irrespective of any program of compulsory contact tracing. Moreover, education as part of a compulsory program has never been demonstrated to be effective.

AIDS and syphilis also have quite different incubation periods. The first symptoms of syphilis—a chancre followed by slight fever and other constitutional symptoms—appear after an incubation period of twelve to thirty days. Symptoms related to HIV infection may not appear for many years, if at all. In most cases, therefore, transmission of HIV infection will very likely have taken place a considerable time before the [infected person] has been identified and his or her contacts have been located.

Despite these obvious limitations, contact tracing might still be a viable policy option if it did not seriously undermine other public health strategies for controlling the spread of AIDS, and if it did not fundamentally affect the rights and dignity of persons vulnerable to HIV infection. Current public health policy is based upon encouraging persons at high risk of contracting HIV infection to voluntarily seek testing to determine their serological status, to have that information reported to public health departments, and then to modify their behavior. The cooperation of persons vulnerable to HIV infection is critical to the achievement of public health objectives.

Contact Tracing

The introduction of contact tracing would significantly interfere with these voluntary strategies for controlling the spread of AIDS. At the heart of voluntarism is trust that the physician/patient relationship will remain confidential and that cooperation will not trigger any form of coercion. The specter of the state interviewing the individual to obtain names and addresses, and then tracing sexual partners and informing them of the person's health status would be regarded as highly intrusive and objectionable. Sexual contact tracing in relation to any disease represents a deep intrusion into individual rights of privacy. But the social dimensions of AIDS are unique in the recent history of disease epidemics. Disclosure by the state that a person has HIV infection can lead to social opprobrium among family and friends, and to loss of employment, housing, and insurance.

The probable outcome of statutorily mandated investigation of sexual contacts, therefore, is that individuals vulnerable to HIV infection would not come forward for testing, impeding

137

epidemiologic and public education efforts; they would not seek counseling, care, and treatment in sexually transmitted disease (STD) and drug dependency clinics, harming these vital public health programs; and they might even refrain from seeking therapeutic treatment for physical illness caused by HIV infection, creating human hardship.

Quarantine Inadequate

There are three ways to protect Americans from the virus. First, government could try to isolate or quarantine the carriers of the disease. Quarantine has been used in previous epidemics, but it is a practical and moral impossibility in the war against AIDS. At least 1.5 million Americans, and possibly twice that number, are now infected with the virus: no conceivable quarantine system would be adequate, and none, given the fearsome medical needs of AIDS patients, would be ethically acceptable. Second, government could try to identify the carriers to the rest of the population. This solution—based on some form of mandatory blood screening—would plainly have Orwellian implications for individual privacy.

The third alternative is to try to eliminate the common behaviors that spread the virus—sharing contaminated needles and having sex without condoms. That means educating both the infected and uninfected sectors of the population about the risks of needles, sex and AIDS. It implies nothing less than a revolution in current sexual mores.

Sharon Begley, *Newsweek*, November 24, 1986.

The justification for sexual contact tracing is based on the right of the state to enter the realm of private affairs for a clear public health benefit, which could override the deep intrusion into individual privacy. Where sexual contact investigation is of marginal public health benefit, or worse, where it may be seriously counterproductive to the achievement of public health goals, it cannot be justified. . . .

Using Isolation

Isolation is the most serious form of deprivation of liberty that can be utilized against a competent and unwilling person. It is based upon what a person *might* do in future rather than what he or she has done; there is no clear temporal limitation; and it is not subject to the same rigorous due process procedures as in a criminal charge.

Given its impact on freedom of movement, isolation is likely to trigger the strictest level of judicial scrutiny. A general isolation of all those who test positive for HIV antibodies or all those with the disease would, in our judgment, be unconstitutional. For every individual who, in fact, poses a danger to public health, many more nondangerous people would be isolated. It is prudent to assume that persons who are seropositive harbor the virus. Yet only a small proportion of this population would be likely intentionally to engage in unsafe sexual behavior or the shared use of contaminated needles, which are the only two efficient mechanisms for HIV transmission. Consequently, isolation would needlessly confine many individuals who are nondangerous.

For many reasons general isolation is not a feasible public health measure to control the spread of HIV infection. First, isolation of the seropositive population would require widespread compulsory public action to reliably locate, identify, and periodically screen persons in high-risk populations. This would involve public resources and invasions of privacy of unacceptable magnitude.

Second, isolation of persons with AIDS or HIV infection would have no finite time limit, because the retrovirus may persist in humans for life. Since there is no therapeutic treatment available, those whose liberty is infringed would have no way to restore themselves to a normal condition in order to rejoin society.

Third, the sheer number of people who harbor the virus, which is estimated at one to two million and rising, would make a general isolation wholly unmanageable.

Finally, since isolation is a civil action that is not intended as a punishment, punitive or unsafe environments would not be legally supportable. Isolated individuals would have to be cared for, treated, fed, and clothed in humane facilities, which currently do not exist. Moreover, reinfection within the segregated facility might be a danger. While scientists do not yet know the factors that cause progression from seropositivity to AIDS, it is possible that repeated exposure to the virus can increase the risk of developing the disease. Isolation in segregated facilities, therefore, may actually pose a danger to the health of those confined.

Limited Isolation

The more serious proposals for isolation do not focus on a person's health status as having a disease or infection, but upon his or her future behavior leading to viral transmission.

A modified isolation statute could require a due process determination that a viral carrier will not, or cannot, refrain from engaging in conduct likely to spread the virus. The 1985 amendment to the Connecticut Public Health Statute, for example, authorizes a local health director to order the confinement of an individual if he has reasonable grounds to believe that the person is infected with a communicable disease and is unable or unwilling to act so as not to expose other persons to infection.

The tension between public health and civil liberties is most apparent when a decision must be taken whether to restrict the freedom of a "recalcitrant" individual, one who intentionally and continuously refuses to comply with reasonable public health directives. The most obvious illustration is a male prostitute with AIDS who reappears at an STD clinic with rectal gonorrhea, despite education and counseling as to the serious consequences of sexual transmission of HIV. Similar situations occur with IV drug users who have to support their dependency by prostitution. . . .

Driving People Underground

In the realm of public health, the most coercive measures may be the *least* effective. Proposals for extreme violations of individual liberties (like quarantine, mass testing or firings) are counterproductive. Such proposals do nothing to stop transmission of the disease, but they do drive people underground. People become afraid to admit having symptoms, to seek testing, or to acknowledge the need to refrain from high-risk behavior.

American Civil Liberties Union, *Civil Liberties*, Winter 1987.

Health officials have a public duty to protect against transmission of a potentially lethal disease agent. Wherever possible, voluntary, or less restrictive compulsory, measures should first be used. But if less restrictive measures were not successful, public health officials would, arguably, be remiss not to exercise the power of limited isolation. Public policy must protect the welfare of those at risk of contracting HIV as well as the civil liberties of those who are infected. Failure to intervene effectively to prevent a serious health hazard does a disservice to those vulnerable to HIV infection.

Nevertheless, a limited use of isolation would prove to be an essentially ineffective and invidious public policy if widely implemented. Proponents see it as an effective method of impeding the spread of the AIDS epidemic. But the invocation of limited isolation does not go to the heart of the epidemic, which cannot be impeded by concentrating on the occasional recalcitrant individual, no matter how dangerous his or her conduct may seem.

Overall, any widespread use of isolation is likely to be counterproductive to the strategy of obtaining voluntary compliance by high-risk group members. As stated previously, any obvious use of coercive measures would tend to discourage persons who are vulnerable to HIV infection from seeking diagnostic testing or treatment, or speaking honestly to counselors concerning their future behavioral intentions. . . .

A limited isolation program based upon preventing intimate personal behavior between two consenting individuals has serious monitoring and enforcement difficulties; it could be viewed as a broad license for public health and law enforcement officials to intrude into the private lives of people vulnerable to HIV infection.

Criminal Law

What role might the criminal law play in identifying behavior resulting in transmission of HIV? It could specifically proscribe behavior likely to communicate HIV infection when a person knows that he or she is infected and appreciates the threat to health or life posed by the behavior, and when he or she does not inform sexual partners of those risks. The knowing or reckless transmission of a potentially lethal infection is just as dangerous as other behavior that the criminal law already proscribes.

This approach cannot be considered unfair to groups at high risk of contracting AIDS, because it serves as a measure of protection for them against the spread of infection. Nor can it be considered unfair to the potential subject of criminal penalties, for it is better to give clear forewarning of unacceptable conduct than to confine a person who might engage in that behavior in the future. . . .

Objection can be made to the use of the criminal law to penalize private sexual activity, particularly when the behavior involves two consenting adults. Yet sexual acts are *not* wholly consensual if the infected person fails to inform his partner of the substantial risk to health; nor is the behavior wholly private because of the public risk inherent in increasing the reservoir of infection. A decision to assume the risk of transferring or contracting a lethal infection clearly concerns members of the public who may become affected. It may be reasonable, therefore, for society to establish clear parameters to behaviors it will not tolerate. By drawing a clear line around the behaviors that pose serious health risks, the law gives notice of the conduct that will be subject to criminal penalty.

However, we do not place any undue reliance upon the criminal law as a mechanism for impeding the spread of HIV infection in the population. Moreover, we have significant reservations about the use of the criminal law in the private realm. . . . It would be virtually impossible to achieve any consistency in application of the criminal law to high-risk behaviors. Variable law enforcement and prosecutorial discretion would result in arbitrary decisions. . . .

Finally, there would be great difficulty in proving beyond a reasonable doubt that a person intentionally or recklessly transmitted the infection. A conviction would have to depend upon the uncorroborated evidence of the person contracting the infection. While similar evidence is used in cases of rape, the person contracting HIV infection would usually not realize that a former sexual partner exposed him or her to the infection until months or years later. It would also have to be demonstrated that the partner was not informed of the risk and that "safe" or "protected" sex, encouraged by CDC, had not taken place. It would be nearly impossible to prove in a courtroom that specific behavior had occurred some time earlier.

The Failure of Compulsion

In the absence of successful behavioral alteration, or scientific intervention, society is beginning to look to the law. There is increasing pressure on public health officials to mark the gravity of the AIDS epidemic by introducing more coercive measures. When dispassionately examined, however, most legal and regulatory proposals would have little, or even a counterproductive, impact on the spread of the HIV infection. They also impose disproportionate restrictions on the liberty, autonomy, and privacy of persons vulnerable to HIV infection. The only conclusion that can be drawn, therefore, is that compulsory legal interventions will not provide a fair and effective means of interrupting the spread of the AIDS epidemic.

Recognizing Deceptive Arguments

People who feel strongly about an issue use many techniques to persuade others to agree with them. Some of these techniques appeal to the intellect, some to the emotions. Many of them distract the reader or listener from the real issues.

Below are listed a few common examples of argumentation tactics. Most of them can be used either to advance an argument in an honest, reasonable way or to deceive or distract from the real issues. It is important for a critical reader to recognize these tactics in order to rationally evaluate an author's ideas.

a. *bandwagon*—the idea that "everybody" does this or believes this

b. *scare tactics*—the threat that if you don't do or don't believe this, something terrible will happen

c. *strawperson*—distorting or exaggerating an opponent's ideas to make one's own seem stronger

d. *personal attack*—criticizing an opponent *personally* instead of rationally debating his or her ideas

e. *testimonial*—quoting or paraphrasing an authority or celebrity to support one's own viewpoint

f. *slanters*—to persuade through inflammatory and exaggerated language instead of reason

g. *generalizations*—using statistics or facts to generalize about a population, place, or thing

h. *categorical statements*—stating something in a way implying that there can be no argument

The following activity will allow you to sharpen your skills in recognizing deceptive reasoning. Some of the statements below are taken from the viewpoints in this chapter. *Beside each one, mark the letter of the type of deceptive appeal being used. More than one type of tactic may be applicable. If you believe the statement is not any of the listed appeals, write N.*

1. Controlling disease by forcing people to change their sexual behavior has never worked.

2. Federal action is essential if the "Typhoid Mikes and Marys" of the AIDS epidemic are to be prevented from continuing to infect others individually and *en masse*.

3. Heterosexuals don't care how many homosexuals die. They just want to keep "their" disease away from "innocent" victims.

4. Because of their outlaw status, IV drug users, prostitutes, and illegal immigrants fear anything that makes them visible to government agencies.

5. Unless drastic measures are taken to prevent the epidemic from spreading, AIDS may well become *everyone's* Final Epidemic.

6. The Centers for Disease Control state that there is little or no risk of contracting AIDS in the workplace. Why, then, do we allow employers to use fear of contagion as an excuse to discriminate against AIDS carriers?

7. In the current political climate, only traditional, god-fearing, Christian family members get equal treatment under the law.

8. High-risk carriers of AIDS are being systematically protected and the lives of countless others put in jeopardy because state and local officials refuse to take effective action to stop its spread.

9. The Justice Department's position is a vicious betrayal of the legal rights of people caught up in the epidemic.

10. Any public health official will tell you that AIDS cannot be spread through casual contact.

11. Homosexuals will go to any length to protect their disease-spreading lifestyle from public scrutiny.

12. If we do not fight the government's efforts to impose mandatory testing, we will soon have to fight to stay out of quarantine camps.

Periodical Bibliography

The following articles have been selected to supplement the diverse views expressed in this chapter.

Glen Allen	''The Ethics of AIDS,'' *Maclean's*, November 18, 1986.
William F. Buckley	''Identify All Carriers,'' *The New York Times*, March 18, 1986.
Fern Schumer Chapman	''AIDS and Business,'' *Fortune*, September 15, 1986.
Matt Clark	''AIDS in the Workplace,'' *Newsweek*, July 7, 1986.
Glamour	''How Companies Are Dealing with AIDS,'' June 1986.
Harper's	''AIDS Outlaws,'' February 1986.
Stephen Koepp	''Living with AIDS on the Job,'' *Time*, August 25, 1986.
Richard Lacayo	''Handicap Rights,'' *Time*, March 16, 1987.
D. Keith Mano	''The Politicization of AIDS,'' *National Review*, February 28, 1986.
The Nation	''Stigmatizing the Victim,'' April 12, 1986.
The Nation	''Unleashing Bias,'' July 5-12, 1986.
National Review	''Gay Rage,'' April 25, 1986.
Nation's Business	''Workplace AIDS,'' November 1986.
Aric Press	''A Victory for AIDS Victims,'' *Newsweek*, March 16, 1987.
David Robinson	''Sodomy and the Supreme Court,'' *Commentary*, November 1986.

Is the Government's Response to AIDS Adequate?

Chapter Preface

The federal government has traditionally contributed to the control of diseases that pose a national health threat. Policies like the one requiring labels on cigarette packages warning of the dangers of smoking help educate the public in ways to avoid disease. Nationwide clinics offer vaccinations against diseases like polio. The rise of AIDS, however, presents a unique challenge to the government in its role as protector of the public health.

One major problem for the government has been in recognizing the extent of the impact of the disease. When AIDS first appeared, it seemed to exclusively affect homosexual males, a social group which did not engender public sympathy in the way that other social groups, such as children, would. Consequently, some critics argue, the government acted too little and too late. It was only when AIDS appeared among the general public, these critics claim, that the government began to take the disease seriously.

The fact that AIDS is transmitted sexually compounds the government's difficulties. The government has found itself trying to educate the public on topics that many Americans are uncomfortable talking about in public, and on which there are deep divisions as to what constitutes appropriate behavior.

As AIDS spreads, the debate about what the government should be doing promises to become even more heated, and the consequences of government action or inaction will affect everyone.

"AIDS is preventable."

The Government Must Respond with Education

C. Everett Koop

On October 22, 1986, C. Everett Koop, the Surgeon General of the United States, issued his official report on AIDS. In the following viewpoint, excerpted from that report, Koop declares that there is no danger of transmission of AIDS through casual contact, and that health officials do not need to carry out mandatory testing or quarantine to control the disease. Instead, according to Koop, the primary response by the government should be to educate the public on how they can voluntarily avoid AIDS. He argues that this information should be given not just to members of AIDS risk groups but to everyone.

As you read, consider the following questions:

1. How does the author think his report can help prevent the disease from spreading?
2. Why is Koop willing to educate the public about safely practicing habits he doesn't approve of such as using illicit drugs?
3. Why does Koop argue that education about AIDS must start during early grade school years?

C. Everett Koop, *Surgeon General's Report on Acquired Immune Deficiency Syndrome*, U.S. Department of Health and Human Services, 1986.

Acquired Immune Deficiency Syndrome is an epidemic that has already killed thousands of people, mostly young, productive Americans. In addition to illness, disability, and death, AIDS has brought fear to the hearts of most Americans—fear of disease and fear of the unknown. Initial reporting of AIDS occurred in the United States, but AIDS and the spread of the AIDS virus is an international problem. This report focuses on prevention that could be applied in all countries. . . .

Controversial Education

The vast majority of Americans are against illicit drugs. As a health officer I am opposed to the use of illicit drugs. As a practicing physician for more than forty years, I have seen the devastation that follows the use of illicit drugs—addiction, poor health, family disruption, emotional disturbances and death. I applaud the President's initiative to rid this nation of the curse of illicit drug use and addiction. The success of his initiative is critical to the health of the American people and will also help reduce the number of persons exposed to the AIDS virus.

Some Americans have difficulties in dealing with the subjects of sex, sexual practices, and alternate lifestyles. Many Americans are opposed to homosexuality, promiscuity of any kind, and prostitution. This report must deal with all of these issues, but does so with the intent that information and education can change individual behavior, since this is the primary way to stop the epidemic of AIDS. This report deals with the positive and negative consequences of activities and behaviors from a health and medical point of view.

Adolescents and pre-adolescents are those whose behavior we wish to especially influence because of their vulnerability when they are exploring their own sexuality (heterosexual or homosexual) and perhaps experimenting with drugs. Teenagers often consider themselves immortal, and these young people may be putting themselves at great risk.

Education about AIDS should start in early elementary school and at home so that children can grow up knowing the behavior to avoid to protect themselves from exposure to the AIDS virus. The threat of AIDS can provide an opportunity for parents to instill in their children their own moral and ethical standards.

Those of us who are parents, educators and community leaders, indeed all adults, cannot disregard this responsibility to educate our young. The need is critical and the price of neglect is high. The lives of our young people depend on our fulfilling our responsibility.

At the beginning of the AIDS epidemic many Americans had little sympathy for people with AIDS. The feeling was that somehow people from certain groups "deserved" their illness. Let us put those feelings behind us. We are fighting a disease, not people. Those who are already afflicted are sick people and need our care as do all sick patients. The country must face this epidemic as a unified society. We must prevent the spread of AIDS while at the same time preserving our humanity and intimacy.

The Issue Is Survival

Let's get it straight. I'm not a moralist, but we have to get the word out in language that is frank enough to be understood. What we're talking about is neither microbes nor morals. We're talking about survival. . . .

This is a very, very tough virus, but we have to muster the will to beat it. Right now, our best weapon is education, and we have to start now to educate the next generation to practice "rational sex" and to stop abusing drugs. Anything less and we're facing disaster.

Norbert Rapoza, PhD, interviewed in *American Medical News,* December 5, 1986.

AIDS is a life-threatening disease and a major public health issue. Its impact on our society is and will continue to be devastating. By the end of 1991, an estimated 270,000 cases of AIDS will have occurred, with 179,000 deaths within the decade since the disease was first recognized. In the year 1991, an estimated 145,000 patients with AIDS will need health and supportive services at a total cost of between $8 and $16 billion. However, AIDS is preventable. It can be controlled by changes in personal behavior. It is the responsibility of every citizen to be informed about AIDS and to exercise the appropriate preventive measures. . . .

The spread of AIDS can and must be stopped. . . .

Risky Behavior

Knowing the facts about AIDS can prevent the spread of the disease. Education of those who risk infecting themselves or infecting other people is the only way we can stop the spread of AIDS. People must be responsible about their sexual behavior and must avoid the use of illicit intravenous drugs and needle sharing. We will describe the types of behavior that lead to infection by the AIDS virus and the personal measures that must be taken for effective protection. If we are to stop the AIDS epidemic, we all must understand the disease—its cause, its nature, and its prevention. *Precautions must be taken.* The AIDS virus infects persons who expose themselves to known risk behavior, such as certain types of homosexual and heterosexual activities or sharing intravenous drug equipment. . . .

Men who have sexual relations with other men are especially

at risk. About 70 percent of AIDS victims throughout the country are male homosexuals and bisexuals. This percentage probably will decline as heterosexual transmission increases. *Infection results from a sexual relationship with an infected person.*

The risk of infection increases according to the number of sexual partners one has, *male or female.* The more partners you have, the greater the risk of becoming infected with the AIDS virus.

Although the AIDS virus is found in several body fluids, a person acquires the virus during sexual contact with an infected person's blood or semen and possibly vaginal secretions. The virus then enters a person's blood stream through their rectum, vagina or penis.

Small (unseen by the naked eye) tears in the surface lining of the vagina or rectum may occur during insertion of the penis, fingers, or other objects, thus opening an avenue for entrance of the virus directly into the blood stream; therefore, the AIDS virus can be passed from penis to rectum and vagina and vice versa without a visible tear in the tissue or the presence of blood.

Couples who maintain mutually faithful monogamous relationships (only one continuing sexual partner) are protected from AIDS through sexual transmission. If you have been faithful for at least five years and your partner has been faithful too, neither of you is at risk. If you have not been faithful, then you and your partner are at risk. If your partner has not been faithful, then your partner is at risk which also puts you at risk. This is true for both heterosexual and homosexual couples. Unless it is possible to know with *absolute certainty* that neither you nor your sexual partner is carrying the virus of AIDS, you must use protective behavior. *Absolute certainty* means not only that you and your partner have maintained a mutually faithful monogamous sexual relationship, but it means that neither you nor your partner has used illegal intravenous drugs.

Preventing Infection—Sex

Some personal measures are adequate to safely protect yourself and others from infection by the AIDS virus and its complications. Among these are:

- If you have been involved in any of the high risk sexual activities described above or have injected illicit intravenous drugs into your body, you should have a blood test to see if you have been infected with the AIDS virus.
- If your test is positive or if you engage in high risk activities and choose not to have a test, you should tell your sexual partner. If you jointly decide to have sex, you must protect your partner by always using a rubber (condom) during (start to finish) sexual intercourse (vagina or rectum).
- If your partner has a positive blood test showing that he/she has been infected with the AIDS virus or you suspect that

151

he/she has been exposed by previous heterosexual or homosexual behavior or use of intravenous drugs with shared needles and syringes, a rubber (condom) should always be used during (start to finish) sexual intercourse (vagina or rectum).

- If you or your partner is at high risk, avoid mouth contact with the penis, vagina, or rectum.
- Avoid all sexual activities which could cause cuts or tears in the linings of the rectum, vagina, or penis.
- Single teenage girls have been warned that pregnancy and contracting sexually transmitted diseases can be the result of only one act of sexual intercourse. They have been taught to say *NO* to sex! They have been taught to say *NO* to drugs! By saying *NO* to sex and drugs, they can avoid AIDS which can *kill* them! The same is true for teenage boys who should also not have rectal intercourse with other males. It may result in AIDS.

© Rosen/Rothco.

- Do not have sex with prostitutes. Infected male and female prostitutes are frequently also intravenous drug abusers; therefore, they may infect clients by sexual intercourse and other intravenous drug abusers by sharing their intravenous drug equipment. Female prostitutes also can infect their unborn babies.

Preventing Infection—Drugs

Drug abusers who inject drugs into their veins are another population group at high risk and with high rates of infection by the AIDS virus. Users of intravenous drugs make up 25 percent of the cases of AIDS throughout the country. The AIDS virus is carried in contaminated blood left in the needle, syringe, or other drug related implements and the virus is injected into the new victim by reusing dirty syringes and needles. Even the smallest amount of infected blood left in a used needle or syringe can contain live AIDS virus to be passed on to the next user of those dirty implements.

No one should shoot up drugs because addiction, poor health, family disruption, emotional disturbances and death could follow. However, many drug users are addicted to drugs and for one reason or another have not changed their behavior. For these people, the only way not to get AIDS is *to use a clean, previously unused* needle, syringe or any other implement necessary for the injection of the drug solution. . . .

What Is Safe?

Everyday living does not present any risk of infection. You *cannot* get AIDS from casual social contact. Casual social contact should not be confused with casual *sexual* contact which is a major cause of the spread of the AIDS virus. Casual *social* contact such as shaking hands, hugging, social kissing, crying, coughing or sneezing, will not transmit the AIDS virus. Nor has AIDS been contracted from swimming in pools or bathing in hot tubs or from eating in restaurants (even if a restaurant worker has AIDS or carries the AIDS virus). AIDS is not contracted from sharing bed linens, towels, cups, straws, dishes, or any other eating utensils. You cannot get AIDS from toilets, doorknobs, telephones, office machinery, or household furniture. You cannot get AIDS from body massages, masturbation or any non-sexual contact.

Donating blood is *not* risky at all. *You cannot get AIDS by donating blood.*

In the U.S. every blood donor is screened to exclude high risk persons and every blood donation is now tested for the presence of antibodies to the AIDS virus. Blood that shows exposure to the AIDS virus by the presence of antibodies is not used either for transfusion or for the manufacture of blood products. Blood banks are as safe as current technology can make them. Because antibodies do not form immediately after exposure to the virus, a newly infected person may unknowingly donate blood after becoming infected but before his/her antibody test becomes positive. It is estimated that this might occur less than once in 100,000.

There is no danger of AIDS virus infection from visiting a doctor, dentist, hospital, hairdresser or beautician. AIDS cannot be transmitted non-sexually from an infected person through a health or service provider to another person. Ordinary methods of disinfection for urine, stool and vomitus which are used for non-infected people are adequate for people who have AIDS or are carrying the AIDS virus. You may have wondered why your dentist wears gloves and perhaps a mask when treating you. This does not mean that he has AIDS or that he thinks you do. He is protecting you and himself from hepatitis, common colds or flu.

There is no danger in visiting a patient with AIDS or caring for him or her. Normal hygienic practices, like wiping of body fluid spills with a solution of water and household bleach (1 part household bleach to 10 parts water), will provide full protection. . . .

The Silence Must End

This silence must end. We can no longer afford to sidestep frank, open discussions about sexual practices whether homosexual or heterosexual. Young men and women will not abstain from sex, and so need direct information about how to enjoy sexual encounters in a reasonably safe and responsible way. They must know and trust their sexual partners, and consistently use a condom during the entire encounter.

Larry Gostin, *Manchester Guardian Weekly*, December 14, 1986.

There are no known cases of AIDS transmission by insects, such as mosquitoes. . . .

Although the AIDS virus has been found in tears and saliva, no instance of transmission from these body fluids has been reported. . . .

Summary of Dangers

AIDS no longer is the concern of any one segment of society; it is the concern of us all. No American's life is in danger if he/she or their sexual partners do not engage in high risk sexual behavior or use shared needles or syringes to inject illicit drugs into the body.

People who engage in high risk sexual behavior or who shoot drugs are risking infection with the AIDS virus and are risking their lives and the lives of others, including their unborn children.

We cannot yet know the full impact of AIDS on our society. From a clinical point of view, there may be new manifestations of AIDS—for example, mental disturbances due to the infection of the brain by the AIDS virus in carriers of the virus. From a social point of view, it may bring to an end the free-wheeling sexual lifestyle which has been called the sexual revolution. Economically, the care of AIDS patients will put a tremendous strain on our already overburdened and costly health care delivery system.

The most certain way to avoid getting the AIDS virus and to control the AIDS epidemic in the United States is for individuals to avoid promiscuous sexual practices, to maintain mutually faithful monogamous sexual relationships and to avoid injecting illicit drugs.

AIDS and the Future

An enormous challenge to public health lies ahead of us and we would do well to take a look at the future. We must be prepared to manage those things we can predict, as well as those we cannot.

At the present time there is no vaccine to prevent AIDS. There is no cure. AIDS, which can be transmitted sexually and by sharing needles and syringes among illicit intravenous drug users, is bound to produce profound changes in our society, changes that will affect us all.

It is estimated that in 1991 54,000 people will die from AIDS. At this moment, many of them are not infected with the AIDS virus. With proper information and education, as many as 12,000 to 14,000 people could be saved in 1991 from death by AIDS.

The changes in our society will be economic and political and will affect our social institutions, our educational practices, and our health care. Although AIDS may never touch you personally, the social impact certainly will.

Be prepared. Learn as much about AIDS as you can. Learn to separate scientific information from rumor and myth. The Public Health Service, your local public health officials and your family physician will be able to help you. . . .

There are a number of people, primarily adolescents, that do not yet know they will be homosexual or become drug abusers and will not heed this message; there are others who are illiterate and cannot heed this message. They must be reached and taught the risk behaviors that expose them to infection with the AIDS virus.

The greatest public health problem lies in the large number of individuals with a history of high risk behavior who have been infected with and may be spreading the AIDS virus. Those with high risk behavior must be encouraged to protect others by adopting safe sexual practices and by the use of clean equipment for intravenous drug use. If a blood test for antibodies to the AIDS virus is necessary to get these individuals to use safe sexual practices, they should get a blood test. Call your local health department for information on where to get the test.

Some people afflicted with AIDS will feel a sense of anger and others a sense of guilt. In spite of these understandable reactions, everyone must join the effort to control the epidemic, to provide for the care of those with AIDS, and to do all we can to inform and educate others about AIDS, and how to prevent it.

Because of the stigma that has been associated with AIDS, many afflicted with the disease or who are infected with the AIDS virus are reluctant to be indentified with AIDS. Because there is no vaccine to prevent AIDS and no cure, many feel there is nothing to be gained by revealing sexual contacts that might also be infected with the AIDS virus. When a community or a state requires reporting of those infected with the AIDS virus to public health authorities in order to trace sexual and intravenous drug contacts—as is the practice with other sexually transmitted diseases—those infected with the AIDS virus go underground out of the mainstream of health care and education. For this reason current public health practice is to protect the privacy of the individual infected with the AIDS virus and to maintain the strictest confidentiality concerning his/her health records. . . .

Education concerning AIDS must start at the lowest grade possible as part of any health and hygiene program. The appearance of AIDS could bring together diverse groups of parents and educators with opposing views on inclusion of sex education in the curricula. There is now no doubt that we need sex education in schools and that it must include information on heterosexual and homosexual relationships. The threat of AIDS should be sufficient to permit a sex education curriculum with a heavy emphasis on prevention of AIDS and other sexually transmitted diseases. . . .

Controversial Issues

A number of controversial AIDS issues have arisen and will continue to be debated largely because of lack of knowledge about AIDS, how it is spread, and how it can be prevented. Among these are the issues of compulsory blood testing, quarantine, and identification of AIDS carriers by some visible sign.

Compulsory blood testing of individuals is not necessary. The procedure could be unmanageable and cost prohibitive. It can be expected that many who *test* negatively might actually be positive due to *recent* exposure to the AIDS virus and give a false sense of security to the individual and his/her sexual partners concerning necessary protective behavior. The prevention behavior described in this report, if adopted, will protect the American public and contain the AIDS epidemic. Voluntary testing will be available to those who have been involved in high risk behavior.

Quarantine has no role in the management of AIDS because AIDS is not spread by casual contact. The only time that some form of quarantine might be indicated is in a situation where an individual carrying the AIDS virus knowingly and willingly continues to expose others through sexual contact or sharing drug equipment. Such circumstances should be managed on a case-by-case basis by local authorities.

Those who suggest the marking of carriers of the AIDS virus by some visible sign have not thought the matter through thoroughly. It would require testing of the entire population which is unnecessary, unmanageable and costly. It would miss those recently infected individuals who would test negatively, but be infected. The entire procedure would give a false sense of security. AIDS must and will be treated as a disease that can infect anyone. AIDS should not be used as an excuse to discriminate against any group or individual.

As the Surgeon General, I will continually monitor the most current and accurate health, medical, and scientific information and make it available to you, the American people. Armed with this information you can join in the discussion and resolution of AIDS-related issues that are critical to your health, your children's health, and the health of the nation.

"We are eager to confront [AIDS] only when it appears at our own doorstep."

Current AIDS Education Efforts Are Inadequate

Robert Bazell and Ronald Moglia

Many government health officials, from the Surgeon General on down, hope that educational efforts will persuade AIDS carriers and those in AIDS risk groups to practice safe sex and take other measures to slow the spread of AIDS. However, some critics charge that current public health efforts at education are inadequate to the task. In Part I of the following viewpoint, Robert Bazell, science reporter for NBC and a columnist with *The New Republic*, claims that the Reagan administration has only paid lip service to the goal of educating the public about AIDS. In Part II, Ronald Moglia, a professor at New York University, insists that the Centers for Disease Control are more concerned with not offending prevailing community standards than they are with educating homosexuals about the dangers of AIDS.

As you read, consider the following questions:

1. According to Bazell, why did the Surgeon General publish a report on AIDS?
2. For what reasons is Bazell hopeful that effective education can control AIDS?
3. Why does Moglia think that efforts by the CDC not to offend the general public with their educational materials for gays are unneccessary?

Robert Bazell, "Surviving AIDS," *The New American*, November 24, 1986. Reprinted by permission of THE NEW REPUBLIC, © 1986, The New Republic, Inc.
Excerpted from Ronald Moglia, "The Safe Sex Shell Game," *SIECUS Report*, vol. 14 no. 5, pp. 15-16. © Sex Information and Education Council of the US. Reprinted by permission.

I

Unless it is possible to know with absolute certainty that your sex partner is not infected with AIDS, through sex or through drug use, you're taking a chance of becoming infected.
—Surgeon General C. Everett Koop

One never knows, do one?

—Fats Waller

The threat of AIDS spreading among heterosexuals who do not inject themselves with drugs—"the general population," in the parlance of many government officials—has returned to the news, as it has from time to time since the disease was recognized five-and-a-half years ago. A report released by the National Academy of Sciences October 29, [1986], "Confronting AIDS," leaves no doubt about the danger. . . . The academy panel detailed a lack of direction and coordination in the federal government's efforts against AIDS. In particular, it described attempts to educate the public about the disease and how to avoid it as "woefully inadequate."

The Koop Report

Dr. Koop released his report in a great hurry the week before, according to people in the Health and Human Services Department, in order to shield himself and his agency from some of the criticism in the academy's study. Indeed, Koop undertook his study only because President Reagan, asked by a reporter what he was doing about AIDS, paused for a long time during which he could not think of anything, and finally replied that he would tell the surgeon general to prepare a report.

In some ways Koop seemed to be favoring an abandonment of sex as the only way to curb the epidemic, but he made some notable distinctions. For example, he recommended that teenage girls should be taught to say no to all sex, whereas teenage boys should merely be warned against having rectal intercourse with other males. Still, most of Koop's calls for education, including more sex education in grade schools, were welcomed by public health officials, if not by other members of the administration. In addition his frank, open language detailing just how the disease spreads differed sharply from previous exercises in mystifying euphemisms.

A National Danger

You would think from the fuss over the academy study and Koop's report that a great, nationwide danger from AIDS had just been discovered. In fact, the warning signs have been glowing brightly for a long time. The Public Health Service estimates that within five years 250,000 people in this country will have been diagnosed with AIDS, and more Americans will be dying of AIDS every year than are now killed annually in traffic accidents or were killed in the entirety of the Vietnam War. But most of those people will be male homosexuals or drug addicts. The best way to get in the news with AIDS or to get Congress and the administration to act is to emphasize the danger to "the general population." Never mind that the disease will kill hundreds of people at the peak of their productive lives. Never mind that each AIDS patient costs taxpayers between $150,000 and $300,000. It seems we are eager to confront a problem only when it appears at our own doorstep. . . .

Government Not Involved

Insofar as changes in sexual behavior can be seen as the problem of a particular community, a fully effective program to alter sexual behavior will involve communal organizations, sex businesses and governments. The reality is that, except for San Francisco, governments at all levels have shown almost total unwillingness to become involved in education about high-risk sex, and while some individual businessmen have shown concern, the overall response of businesses has been spasmodic and half-hearted. Where education goes on at all it is because gay organizations—political, medical and welfare—have taken on the job and pushed businesses and governments for support.

Dennis Altman, *AIDS in the Mind of America*, 1986.

The evidence is already accumulating. For more than a year the armed forces have been testing all recruits for antibodies to the AIDS virus. Nationwide, one out of 2,000 recruits tests positive. But in areas where there is already a lot of AIDS, the rates are much higher. In New York City and San Francisco, one out of 100 tests positive. For recruits from Manhattan the rate is one in 50. It appears that most of them are neither intravenous drug users nor homosexuals. They are just ghetto kids. The danger remains that poor minorities will not be seen as part of that all-important "general public," and that prevention efforts in those areas will be too little and too late. . . .

The course that AIDS has followed in Haiti may serve as an . . . important warning. AIDS appeared in Haiti about the same time it appeared in the United States. The first cases were among bisexual men who worked as prostitutes servicing American and European tourists. From the bisexuals it spread quickly through sex and by blood transfusion to others in the population. In 1981 12 percent of the AIDS cases in Haiti were females. Now women account for 40 percent of the cases.

It is likely that AIDS spread so quickly among heterosexuals in Haiti because of promiscuity. Polygamy is common, and among the very poor sex is the only activity that is free and enjoyable. In addition, the terrible poverty forces many women to sell themselves. But just because it spread faster in Haiti does not mean it could not spread in the same way here. . . .

Urgent Need for Education

Statements from administration officials, particularly Margaret Heckler when she was secretary of health and human services, could give you the idea that technology is racing to the rescue and we will have a cure or a vaccine within a few years. Asked about that at his recent news conference, Dr. Koop said, "That idea went to Ireland with Mrs. Heckler." The truth is that while scientists have learned an enormous amount about the AIDS virus, they have also found that it is one of the most complex infectious agents they have ever encountered. A treatment or a vaccine is many, many years away.

So education is our best bet. Everyone, particularly sexually active youngsters, should know that having sex without a condom and/or spermicidal jelly (which can help prevent a woman from being infected) is risking your life. The danger in the ghetto is great already. Among the middle class the risk is less, but it increases daily. . . .

In many ways the task of stopping AIDS is simple in the United States compared to other places, such as Africa and Haiti, where the disease is widespread. We have a literate population, and there is an excellent chance education can be effective. Dr. Mann of the World Health Organization is also optimistic about the chances in other parts of the world. "Cultures," he said, "know how to survive. Societies know how to survive. And when faced with a threat to their young and previously healthy men and women, cultures will find ways to adapt." We can only hope that such optimism is justified.

II

In this time, with the Reagan Administration's emphasis on national defense spending and lack of appropriations for social and health issues, many sexuality programs are being forced to cut services. However, there is apparently one exception to that national policy. The Administration has verbalized its recognition of the importance of appropriating the funds needed to combat the potential spread of AIDS through sexual contact within the gay population. . . .

AIDS Education: A Priority

In a recent document the Centers for Disease Control put forth its argument for funding these educational programs. CDC stated that "the current lack of therapeutic or vaccine methods to control the spread of HTLV-III/LAV virus infection and AIDS requires *the promotion of sexual and lifestyle behaviors for individuals to reduce their risk of acquiring and spreading the virus* [author's emphasis]. Behavioral science research suggests that expecting people to permanently alter any set of behaviors affecting their health is unrealistic unless the educational message provides acceptable alternatives to the behavior creating the risk. Consequently, AIDS risk reduction efforts have focused on the promotion of responsible sex practices for individuals, such as gay and bisexual men, for whom sexual activity is an important factor of risk in acquiring or spreading HTLV-III/LAV" [HIV].

It is encouraging to note that one branch of this anti-sex education administration has realized the value of education and even has asked for proposals from sexuality professionals in an attempt to halt the spread of this health problem. Indeed, CDC goes on to enunciate a rationale that many sex educators could adopt for encouraging development of other sex education programs: "The adoption of 'safer sex' practices is a practical concept of AIDS risk reduction and is being suggested as a strategy intended to minimize the spread of HTLV-III/LAV infection among sexually active individuals, including gay and bisexual men. Implementing programs to promote a 'safer sex' risk reduction strategy may involve supporting the communication of suggestions using candid terms, some of which may provoke criticism in society."

Say No or Die?

Many continue to focus on sexual morality instead of the deadly amorality of a virus. We have not yet made a crucial shift in our priorities, putting health first. . . .

There are some who offer a one-word answer to this epidemic: no. Say no to unwed sex. Say no to prostitution. Say no to drugs. But is this to be our sole national-health program: "Say No or Die"? And how do we protect people from those who said "yes"?

Ellen Goodman, *St. Paul Pioneer Press Dispatch,* January 27, 1987.

CDC seems to be acknowledging that many of the practices of this sub-group of the population may not be understood or even acceptable to the majority of the national public. This seems a logical conclusion, since many Americans view homosexuality as an offensive, unnatural act. Even among the more enlightened of the heterosexual public, the frequency of anal intercourse is vastly lower than in the gay population. Therefore, CDC is absolutely correct in the assumption that there are many intrinsic differences between the groups.

Nevertheless, CDC states that this heterosexual group will be the final judge for evaluating what should be included in these educational programs for the gay population. Their guidelines state: "Such terms or descriptors used should be those which a reasonable person would conclude should be understood by a *broad cross section of educated adults in society*, or which when used to communicate with a specific group, like gay men about high risk sexual practices, would be judged by a reasonable person to be *unoffensive to the most educated adults BEYOND THE GROUP*" [author's emphasis].

CDC then goes on to discuss the importance of not using audiovisual material that may be offensive. They are more explicit in this restriction: "Audiovisual materials and pictorials in addition should communicate risk reduction messages by inference rather than through any display of the anogenital area of the body or overt depiction of the performance of 'safer sex' or 'unsafe sex' practices." One can only surmise that CDC's logic must be that the educational value of "overt depiction" illustrations is not as important as the potential offensiveness to the populations *beyond the group*, who will never see them! . . .

Programs Out of Touch

The overseers of these guidelines are a panel of good citizens who are in touch with the "prevailing community standards." This panel "of no less than five persons representing a reasonable cross section of the general community, *not drawn predominantly from the target group*" will review and approve the proposal submissions incuding all "written materials, pictorials, and audiovisuals and proposed educational group session activities" [author's emphasis]. Dr. Michael Quadland, a respected authority of sex education programs for the gay population, points out "that any government-backed programs directed toward other minorities, such as blacks or Hispanics, is usually administered by a majority of the particular groups and that the language used in public education is usually directed toward the target group."

These guidelines have put sexuality education organizations in a dilemma. They need this funding to develop and conduct safe sex programs, but are ethically strained to tailor their programs to CDC's restrictions. Is it possible that CDC has not heard of the President's firm commitment to preventing and conquering this disease? Or are the President's public statements examples of what Mark Twain called *petrified truth?*

> *"It is absurd to claim that 'value judgments are absent' in [AIDS education] classes. Of course* values *are imparted—perverse values!"*

Current AIDS Education Efforts Promote Immorality

William F. Jasper and Kirk Kidwell

In his report on AIDS, Surgeon General C. Everett Koop called for teaching children as early as the third grade how AIDS is spread and how to avoid it. In Part I of the following viewpoint, William F. Jasper, contributing editor to *The New American*, argues that teaching about AIDS will mean giving classroom instruction in immoral sexual practices. In Part II, Kirk Kidwell, Washington correspondent for *The New American*, states that government reliance on sex education in schools to control AIDS will not work.

As you read, consider the following questions:

1. What might be taught as part of an AIDS education program, according to Jasper?
2. How does Jasper think national health and education organizations will get around local objections to the content of their sex education programs?
3. What lesson, according to Kidwell, should educators learn from their previous experience with sex education? Do you agree with his conclusion? Why or why not?

William F. Jasper, "Teaching AIDS," *The New American*, December 22, 1986. Reprinted with permission.
Kirk Kidwell, "AIDS Education for Your 3rd Grader?" *The New American*, November 24, 1986. Reprinted with permission.

"The threat of AIDS should be sufficient to permit a sex education curriculum with a heavy emphasis on prevention of AIDS and other sexually transmitted diseases," said U.S. Surgeon General C. Everett Koop at his October 22nd [1986] news conference coinciding with the release of his long-awaited report on AIDS. According to his report, "There is no doubt that we need sex education in schools and that it must include information on heterosexual and homosexual relationships." Furthermore, "AIDS education must start at the lowest grade possible." According to Dr. Koop, third grade may not be too early.

Media Supports AIDS Education

The following week, on October 29th, the National Academy of Sciences released its 390-page study, "Confronting AIDS," which states: "Schools have an obligation to provide sex and health education, including facts about AIDS, in terms that teenagers can understand."

Both the Koop and NAS reports have received (and continue to receive) extensive, favorable media coverage by the major press and the television/radio networks. Coincidentally, while the public was being peppered with "news" stories on the alleged need for more comprehensive sex education to avert a national "catastrophe," Planned Parenthood launched its Madison Avenue advertising campaign featuring full-page ads in major newspapers and magazines lobbying for increased sex ed programs and school-based clinics to dispense contraceptives and abortion information.

As you would expect, in the midst of all of this a Gallup Poll was produced showing that American parents "overwhelmingly" support the idea of AIDS education as part of a comprehensive sex ed program in the schools. And why not? After all, we are told that it has been endorsed by the National School Boards Association. And Dr. Koop's report was made "in consultation with" the National PTA, the National Association of Elementary School Principles and other august-sounding educational bodies.

What Will Be Taught?

But do parents and educators know what they are getting into— or, rather, what they are getting their children into? The Koop report calls for "frank, open discussions about sexual practices— homosexual and heterosexual," while the NAS study says education "must be as direct as possible" and must "use whatever vernacular is required." But, for all the talk about being open and direct, both reports are exceedingly vague about *who* should be taught *what* and by *whom*.

At his October 22nd press conference, Dr. Koop told the nation: "This is an objective health and medical report.... Value

Mike Shelton. Reprinted with special permission of King Features Syndicate, Inc.

judgments are absent." Great pains are taken to skirt any mention of right or wrong. Homosexuality and premarital sex are accepted as alternative lifestyles. This is hardly surprising considering that the National Gay Task Force and other homosexual organizations were consulted in the preparation of this study, and their addresses and phone numbers are listed for additional reference in the back of the booklet. The report's recommendations are purely mechanistic: limit your number of sexual partners (homosexual and heterosexual) and use a condom to reduce your chances of contracting AIDS. Simply put, the emphasis is on promoting "safe" sodomy and fornication. It is absurd to claim that "value judgments are absent" in such classes. Of course *values* are imparted—*perverse values!* To be fair, the Koop report does advise that "By saying NO to sex and drugs, they [teenage girls] can avoid AIDS which can *kill* them! The same is true for teenage boys who should also not have rectal intercourse with other males. It may result in AIDS." But even this seemingly forthright morally-tinged advice is a mere mechanistic, medical admonition. Besides, it is lost among the 36 pages of "non-judgmental" text.

Just how "explicit" will these AIDS/sex ed classes get? Again, our "open, frank" *experts* refuse to say. The Koop booklet quite explicitly defines oral and anal sexual contact, using terminology

166

that we are reluctant to print in this magazine. Is this what our 3rd-grade children will discuss? Or 5th grade, or 9th grade? Or will they be shown films or other audio-visual aids so that they understand these various "sexual contacts"? Will homosexual activists be brought to school to explain (advocate) the alternative lifestyle? Will 6th graders sit around in a circle and chant in unison the four-letter "street" words for reproductive organs and sexual activities to get rid of sexual "hangups" and enable better communication?

Don't roll your eyes. Much of this already is being done in schools all across the country. No one was "available" at the Surgeon General's office for comment. Dr. Sheldon Wolff, co-chairman of the NAS committee that issued the AIDS report, told *The New American* that AIDS/sex ed classes "would not promote homosexuality" nor encourage "sexual experimentation."

More Big Government

He was able to offer this assurance even though he said that the NAS was not involved with any specific course content. According to the NAS study, "The most fundamental obligation for AIDS education rests with the federal government," so the Academy recommends establishing a new federal bureaucracy to implement this. The NAS report expresses concern about local groups reviewing curricular materials to see that community standards are not violated. This could destroy educational effectiveness! NAS' AIDS co-chairman Dr. David Baltimore is concerned that undue worry over the so-called "dirty word" syndrome might lead educators to shy away from explicit materials in AIDS classes.

The NAS' solution? "If government agencies continue to be unable or unwilling to use direct, explicit terms in the detailed content of educational programs," says the report, "contractual arrangements should be established with *private organizations that are not subject to the same inhibitions*" (our emphasis). Such as the National Gay Task Force, Planned Parenthood, the North American Man-Boy Love Association?

II

The only answer to the spread of AIDS, public health experts tell us, is education. "Knowing the facts about AIDS can prevent the spread of the disease," suggests the Surgeon General's Report on AIDS. "Education of those who risk infecting themselves or infecting other people is the *only* way we can stop the spread of AIDS." (Emphasis added.)

Yet, educating only those currently at risk for AIDS is not enough, in the Surgeon General's opinion. "Education about AIDS should start at an early age so that children can grow up knowing the behaviors to avoid to protect themselves from exposure to the

AIDS virus," Surgeon General C. Everett Koop explained. "AIDS education must start at the lowest grade possible as part of any health and hygiene program. There is now no doubt that we need sex education in schools and that it includes information on sexual practices that may put our children at risk for AIDS."

But is a massive AIDS education program in public schools (beginning in the third grade, as Dr. Koop later suggested) really the answer? Judging from the record of 15 years of sex education and family planning in the schools—initially proposed as *the* solution to teenage pregnancy—the answer to that question is most emphatically, "No."

Sex Education a Failure

According to a study published in the journal *Family Perspective*, sex education and family planning programs have actually increased teenage pregnancy. "In fact, direct empirical estimates . . . showed greater family planning involvement to be associated with higher, not lower teenage pregnancy rates," write researchers Stan E. Weed and Joseph A. Olsen of the Institute for Research and Evaluation in Salt Lake City, Utah. "[I]nstead of the expected reductions in overall pregnancy and abortion rates, teenage family planning program participation was associated with higher rates of both pregnancy and abortion."

No Safe Sex

There simply isn't any "safe" sex for schoolchildren. Courses and teachers that instruct otherwise are betraying the confidence that parents and the public have put in them in entrusting children to their care. Schoolchildren should be taught to practice abstinence until marriage and fidelity after marriage, and to expect your future spouse to do likewise.

Phyllis Schlafly, *The Phyllis Schlafly Report*, February 1987.

Writing in the *Wall Street Journal*, Dr. Weed noted that "family planning for teen-agers is clearly not the first federal effort to be less successful than hoped nor the first to have effects other than those intended. . . . The medical/technical solution of 'responsible contraceptive behavior' appeared to be a simple and straightforward solution to a pressing public health problem. It was assumed that a trend toward greater sexual activity was inevitable and irreversible and that providing relevent information and contraceptives would be the optimal response. It hasn't been."

The public health experts were flat wrong about teenage pregnancy. They reasoned that, since it was inevitable that teenagers were going to experiment with sex, the only solution was to educate them on avoiding the risks of pregnancy. Their solution—sex education and free access to family planning clinics—has not solved the teenage pregnancy crisis; it has only made matters worse.

Same Mistake with AIDS

Unfortunately, it appears that the public health experts are making the same mistake with regard to AIDS. Proclaiming the inevitability of sex apart from heterosexual matrimony, the experts are proposing AIDS education and free access to condoms as the *only* answer to this public health crisis.

It is time for the experts to learn from their past mistakes. AIDS education, like sex education, is not the answer. Barring transmission through blood products, people do not become infected with the AIDS virus through ignorance. Rather, neglecting the information already available, they willfully engage in practices they know to be dangerous. The answer is not education and condoms, but chastity before marriage (between a man and woman) and marital faithfulness.

"We need to take bold actions to provide desperately needed treatment to those who are otherwise doomed."

The FDA Should Make AIDS Drugs More Available

Mathilde Krim and Dale Gieringer

Several drugs have been developed that may help in the treatment of AIDS. However, most of these drugs have not gone through the Food and Drug Administration's long and rigorous approval process. In the following two-part viewpoint, Mathilde Krim and Dale Gieringer argue for making experimental drugs more quickly available to informed patients. Krim is a research biologist at St. Luke's/Roosevelt Hospital Center and Columbia University's College of Physicians and Surgeons. Gieringer is a policy analyst with the Decisions and Ethics Center of Stanford University.

As you read, consider the following questions:

1. According to Krim, at what point should a new AIDS drug be tested on AIDS patients and those infected with the AIDS virus?
2. Why, according to Gieringer, is the FDA's "compassionate use" approval procedure inadequate?
3. What advantages does Gieringer see in allowing experimental drugs to be used by consumers who have given informed consent?

Mathilde Krim, "A Chance at Life for AIDS Sufferers," *The New York Times*, August 8, 1986. Copyright © 1986 by The New York Times Company. Reprinted by permission. Dale Gieringer, "Twice Wrong on AIDS," *The New York Times*, January 12, 1987. Copyright © 1987 by The New York Times Company. Reprinted by permission.

I

We need to take bold actions to provide desperately needed treatment to those who are otherwise doomed. One step would be to make available experimental drugs. While scientists test new drugs that offer glimmers of hope, the victims of this disease must wait years, because it is not economical for companies to develop new drugs. Unfortunately, these gravely ill people do not have years to wait. The Federal Government should issue contracts to drug companies for fast production of experimental drugs.

Time-Consuming Procedure

In order to protect its citizens from exposure to drugs that may do more harm than good, this nation has wisely established a cautious, orderly and time-consuming procedure for the scientific evaluation of all new pharmaceutical products before they can be placed on the market. The Food and Drug Administration oversees the approval procedure, which can take more than five years, and the agency generally will not permit the release of a promising drug before it is formally licensed and approved.

But exemptions are allowed for the treatment of serious diseases for which there is no accepted form of therapy, such as certain forms of advanced cancer. The range of doses within which the drug is not overly toxic must be determined and some evidence must exist showing that there is reason to think it might fight the disease. How much toxicity is acceptable? How thin can the thread of preliminary, but encouraging, results be? These considerations are balanced against the life-threatening nature of the disease if left untreated.

As soon as it can be determined that new drugs meet the requirements of the F.D.A.'s exemption guidelines, they should be released for limited use. . . .

Need More Trials

Based on our emerging knowledge of the natural course of the infection, it is likely that any treatment at the early stages of the illness for those whose immune defense system still has some regenerative capacity would stand the best chance of producing beneficial and discernible results. Thus, once pilot studies on a drug that may be effective against AIDS have established the dose range that falls within tolerable toxicity levels, carefully controlled trials for efficacy should be conducted on patients with AIDS-related complex, or possibly even on patients who are merely infected but who show no signs of illness.

This does not mean abandoning patients who suffer from the end stage of the disease. Patients with very limited time to live, and the physicians who care for them, should be entitled to access to any experimental drug that offers hope—no matter how slim that hope may be.

171

Permitting physicians to use experimental drugs to treat patients whose lives are in immediate jeopardy should not be done out of a wishful belief that the treatment would work. It should be done out of respect for the patient's right to fight for life with whatever tools we can offer.

Currently, the only way an AIDS patient can obtain the most promising antiviral and other experimental therapies is to be enrolled in one of the controlled clinical trials conducted at academic medical centers. Even taking into account the enlarged enrollment made possible by 14 new AIDS treatment units, only 10 percent of AIDS patients can hope to be accepted into these clinics.

Denying Life-Saving Drugs

Since the disfiguring thalidomide disaster among newborns in the early 1960s, drug regulators have been extremely cautious, less because they feared science than because they feared Congress's penchant for publicly humiliating federal workers. Those injured by adverse drug reactions are painfully obvious; those helped by new drugs are obscure even if far more numerous. Not only has the FDA been seeking risk-free drugs, it also has been applying the most rigorous methods of science to decide on the efficacy of each new drug. The result has been to deny patients modern therapy even when it might save their lives. Every time a hopeful new drug is reported, patients are told it is "years away."

Editorial, *The Wall Street Journal*, March 13, 1987.

The costs exceed $10,000 a year for each patient, and to make experimental drugs available to 18,000 patients through clinical trials would cost more than $180 million in the first year. In addition to being very costly, clinical treatment would also be virtually impossible logistically. As a result, 90 percent of AIDS patients now receive no treatment at all for their underlying infection. As the number of cases increases, as it surely will, the possibility of accommodating a larger proportion of AIDS patients in clinical trials can only decrease.

If the F.D.A. released experimental drugs for only those patients who are severely ill, it would not prevent continued, carefully controlled investigations on those drugs. The most valuable proof of the efficacy of the drugs will come from studies conducted on patients in the earlier stages of illness. Qualified physicians should be given access to the safest and most promising experimental drugs.

It may be necessary to subsidize the production of certain drugs, and it is imperative that physicians selected to receive the drugs be given instruction on their safe use and on monitoring possible undesirable side effects. The Government would have to give money to these efforts, but it would be a fraction of the cost of enrolling all AIDS patients in controlled research trials.

Entitled to Hope

Patients with cancer and other life-threatening diseases for which there is no established therapy can avail themselves of the latest, most hopeful treatments, even if they are still experimental. Americans who have AIDS should be entitled to the same measure of hope. It has been said: "Without hope, the heart would break." As things stand now, the heart does break.

II

Food and Drug Administration regulations are designed to deny access to potentially life-saving drugs. Under present law, no new drug or medical device can be marketed until it has been officially approved as "safe and effective" by the F.D.A.

F.D.A. approval is a lengthy process that routinely takes years to complete. At least 70 percent of new drugs are approved in foreign countries before the United States approves them, often by many months or years.

Access Limited

Prior to approval, drugs can be used only in investigational studies that have been specifically pre-approved by the F.D.A. through a procedure known as IND—for "investigational drug" —approval.

Because investigational drug requirements are stringent, time-consuming and expensive, access to unapproved drugs is severely limited. Of the nation's estimated 28,000 AIDS victims—living and dead—only a few hundred have been accepted in F.D.A.-approved drug studies. Most of these have been "double-blind" studies: half of the subjects receive nothing more than a placebo.

Occasionally, the F.D.A. allows "compassionate use" of investigational drugs for patients with otherwise hopeless conditions. However, the agency's definition of compassion is scarcely generous. Last year, the F.D.A. refused a compassionate-use permit for a temporary artificial heart in a 33-year-old patient dying of heart failure. Aside from AZT, no AIDS drugs are available on a compassionate-use basis.

Compassionate use involves burdensome red tape and paperwork. Thus, many physicians are reluctant to apply for it for their patients. In 1985, the Food and Drug Administration announced it would permit compassionate use of the drug isoprinosine, an immune booster of possible benefit for AIDS. But the manufacturer, Newport Pharmaceuticals, could not afford to make it available because the cost of complying with F.D.A. regulations came to some $2,000 per patient. In comparison, a year's supply of isoprinosine could be bought from Newport's Mexican subsidiary for only $300.

The perverse result of the F.D.A.'s "protection" has been that American patients have been forced to seek treatment abroad. Hundreds of AIDS victims have been going to Mexico for isoprinosine and ribavarin, another unapproved drug with some potential for mitigating AIDS.

Informed Consent

Reform is needed to allow patients freedom of access to experimental drugs. The basic idea should be to legalize use of unapproved drugs so long as patients receive appropriate warnings to insure informed consent. Unproved or hazardous drugs should be clearly distinguished through label and oral warnings, with signed informed consent statements where necessary to insure that no one is exposed to them involuntarily.

Roll Call of Death

Many of us who live in daily terror of the AIDS epidemic cannot understand why the Food and Drug Administration has been so intransigent in the face of this monstrous tidal wave of death. Its response to what is plainly a national emergency has been inadequate, its testing facilities are inefficient and gaining access to its staff and activities is virtually impossible. One private doctor, anticipating the F.D.A.'s release of the drug AZT, said that it would amount to a "sop to the gay community—so they'll shut up. They can't say they haven't been given *something.*"

Indeed, these are understatements. There is no question on the part of anyone fighting AIDS that the F.D.A. constitutes the single most incomprehensible bottleneck in American bureaucratic history— one that is actually prolonging this roll call of death.

Larry Kramer, *The New York Times*, March 23, 1987.

Informed choice would enhance drug safety by giving consumers better information about drug risks. Americans are now among the least well-informed drug consumers in the world. Dangerous prescription drugs are commonly sold without any label instructions or warnings. There is reason to think that the misuse of existing old drugs is a greater health hazard than exposure to new, untested ones. Under an informed-choice system, consumers of new and old drugs alike would receive suitable warnings and usage instructions.

"Without methodical testing, there is no way to learn whether such drugs prolong life or merely stretch out a painful dying process."

The FDA Should Not Make AIDS Drugs More Available

Daniel S. Greenberg

The federal government's Food and Drug Administration must approve every new drug before it can be sold in the US. The process for approving a drug can take years. With the advent of AIDS, the FDA is being pressured to speed up the approval process so that experimental drugs can be given to AIDS patients who otherwise have little hope of improvement. But in the following viewpoint, Daniel S. Greenberg argues that the FDA is practicing misguided compassion for AIDS patients by allowing them to use untested, potentially useless or even harmful, drugs. Greenberg is the publisher and editor of *Science and Government Report* and writes a syndicated column on science and health policy.

As you read, consider the following questions:

1. What does the author think of the results of the testing done on azidothymidine (AZT)?
2. According to the author, what is the cause of the FDA's seeming sluggishness in approving new AIDS drugs?
3. What parallel does Greenberg see between the new AIDS drugs and the cancer drug Interleukin-2?

Daniel S. Greenberg, "The government bends to AIDS victim's pleas," *U.S. News & World Report*, March 23, 1987. Reprinted with the author's permission.

AIDS patients are going to die anyway. Why not let them have any medicine that might possibly help?

The Food and Drug Administration, long accused of bureaucratic sluggishness, has now responded sympathetically to that anguished question. On March 10 [1987], the FDA announced its intent to give private doctors access to drugs that show some promise of helping desperately sick patients—even before long and methodical clinical trials are complete. The proposal is indisputably humane in intent and fulfills the public's clear desire to mobilize everything possible against the AIDS scourge. But hastening the release of new drugs will worsen the dilemma rather than resolve it.

So far, none of the few experimental drugs works well. Some don't work at all. Worse, their unrestricted use would disrupt attempts to find better ones. With the epidemic continuing its deadly spread, impulses toward quick fixes must be checked.

Some experimental drugs do exist that seem to postpone death, at least for a while, for some patients. Among them is the highly publicized antiviral compound AZT, or azidothymidine. In controlled tests last year, only one death occurred among 145 AIDS patients receiving AZT over eight months, compared with 16 deaths among 137 patients on placebo pills. The tests were skimpy by the usual standards of pharmaceutical evaluation, and it was clear that in some patients AZT produces such devastating side effects, including anemia and high fevers, that prolonged use would be intolerable. Even so, in the face of tangible results, the placebo tests were discontinued as ethically indefensible.

On a Fast Track

Unofficially, the FDA already had put AIDS drugs on a faster-than-usual track. Burroughs Wellcome, the pharmaceutical firm that holds the patent on AZT, began testing it on people in 1985. In September of 1986, the FDA halted the clinical trials. The company was allowed to furnish the drug, free, to private doctors to give to patients suffering from *Pneumocystis carinii* pneumonia, which kills people whose immune systems have been destoyed by AIDS. In January, 1987, an FDA advisory panel recommended that AZT be approved for sale against both *Pneumocystis carinii* pneumonia and advanced AIDS-related complex (ARC), which can be a precursor of full-fledged AIDS. The FDA hasn't acted, but in the light of its March 10 proposal it would be shocking if the panel's advice were rejected. The approval would reduce by two or three years the time it otherwise might take for these patients to get the drug.

At the urging of gay activists and many physicians, the FDA now would go further—releasing AZT and other experimental drugs to dying patients who may have neither *Pneumocystis carinii* pneumonia nor ARC. On balance, given the bleak fate awaiting these patients, the FDA has no choice. But AZT is a shot in the dark, of uncertain value, and its hurried release will not help provide what's most needed in the AIDS crisis—hard data. Without methodical testing, there is no way to learn whether such drugs prolong life or merely stretch out a painful dying process. If indeed they have long-term value, only careful tests can determine the proper dosages for the proper patients.

Need Proof That Drugs Work

Some AIDS victims are demanding access to experimental drugs on the ground that, since they are dying, they have nothing to lose. But a drug can best be tested by comparing a group of people who are taking it with a control group of people who are not. If drugs that are being tested become widely available, it will be difficult to recruit volunteers for control groups, and that could delay for years proof that a drug really works.

Peter Nolty, *Fortune*, September 15, 1986.

Impatience with the slow-moving FDA is understandable. But the sluggishness arises from the immense difficulties in sorting out interactions between sick people and complicated chemicals. The most dangerous element in that process is desperate hope, not bureaucratic perversity. . . .

The argument against letting misguided compassion force the release of anti-AIDS drugs prematurely was clearly stated last year in congressional testimony by Dr. Martin Hirsch of Massachusetts General Hospital: "Release of any drug prior to demonstration of clear clinical benefit would make it impossible to conduct properly controlled trials of drug safety and efficacy, thus only delaying licensure of effective therapeutic agents." The sensible goal, Hirsch said, should be more trials of drugs on patients. Hasty approval of unproven drugs, he said, "would only create false hopes and delay accumulation of accurate knowledge that would save lives."

More and more drugs and AIDS patients are being enrolled in such trials, but the experimental process remains unavoidably slow. There is a ring of humanity in the calls for wider use of AZT and other AIDS drugs. But it is a false ring.

Recognizing Statements That Are Provable

From various sources of information we are constantly confronted with statements and generalizations about social and moral problems. In order to think clearly about these problems, it is useful to be able to make a basic distinction between statements for which evidence can be found and other statements which cannot be verified or proved because evidence is not available or the issue is too controversial.

Readers should constantly be aware that magazines, newspapers, and other sources often contain statements of a controversial or questionable nature. The following activity is designed to allow experimentation with statements that are provable and those that are not.

Most of the following statements are derived from the viewpoints in this chapter. Consider each statement carefully. *Mark P for any statement you believe is provable. Mark U for any statement you feel is unprovable because of the lack of evidence. Mark C for any statements you think are too controversial to be proved to everyone's satisfaction.*

If you are doing this activity as a member of a class or group, compare your answers with those of other class or group members. Be able to defend your answers. You may discover that others will come to different conclusions than you. Listening to the reasons others present for their answers may give you valuable insights in recognizing statements that are provable.

If you are reading this book alone, ask others if they agree with your answers. You too will find this interaction valuable.

P = *provable*
U = *unprovable*
C = *too controversial*

1. The President's initiative to rid this nation of the curse of illicit drug use and addiction will help reduce the number of persons exposed to the AIDS virus.

2. It is the responsibility of every citizen to be informed about AIDS and to exercise the appropriate preventive measures.

3. Quarantine has no role in the management of AIDS because AIDS is not spread by casual contact.

4. Each AIDS patient costs taxpayers between $150,000 and $300,000.

5. In many ways the task of stopping AIDS is simple in the United States.

6. The overseers of the safe sex guidelines at the Centers for Disease Control are a panel of good citizens who are in touch with the prevailing community standards.

7. The best way to get Congress to act on AIDS is to emphasize the danger to the general population.

8. AIDS prevention efforts for ghetto kids will be too little and too late.

9. Dr. Koop's calls for education to control the spread of AIDS were welcomed by public health officials.

10. Schools have an obligation to provide facts about AIDS in terms that teenagers can understand.

11. The emphasis of the Koop report is on promoting safe sodomy and fornication.

12. The most fundamental obligation for AIDS education rests with the federal government.

13. Chastity before marriage and marital faithfulness will work better to prevent AIDS than education programs.

14. Worry over the so-called "dirty word" syndrome will lead educators to shy away from explicit materials in AIDS classes.

15. The Food and Drug Administration will not permit the release of a promising drug before it is formally licensed and approved.

16. Ninety percent of AIDS patients now receive no treatment at all for their underlying infection.

17. Patients with cancer can avail themselves of the latest treatments even if they are still experimental.

Periodical Bibliography

The following articles have been selected to supplement the diverse views expressed in this chapter.

Lawrence K. Altman   "Cooperation vs. Competition," *The New York Times*, April 14, 1987.

Christianity Today   "Addressing the AIDS Threat," December 23, 1985.

Matt Clark   "Uproar over AIDS Drugs," *Newsweek*, April 6, 1987.

Forbes   "Bucking the Bureaucrats," March 24, 1986.

Denise Grady   "Look, Doctor, I'm Dying. Give Me the Drug," *Discover*, August 1986.

Harper's   "AIDS: What Is To Be Done?" forum, October 1985.

Peter Huber   "AIDS and Lawyers," *The New Republic*, May 5, 1986.

Ed Magnuson   "Taking His Own Medicine," *Time*, March 30, 1987.

Colleen O'Connor   "Koop Makes Waves in His War on AIDS," *Newsweek*, March 2, 1987.

B.J. Phillips   "Fateful Decisions on Treating AIDS," *Time*, February 2, 1987.

Julia Reed   "The Hot New Politics of AIDS," *U.S. News & World Report*, March 30, 1987.

Joanne Silberner   "AIDS Drug Approval Recommended," *Science News*, January 24, 1987.

USA Today   "Efforts To Control AIDS Epidemic Hampered," October 1986.

Amy Wilentz   "A Transfusion of Fear," *Time*, March 30, 1987.

How Will AIDS Affect Society?

Chapter Preface

In a 1985 *Time* magazine essay, Lance Morrow states that among the general public the fear of AIDS is rivaled only by the fear of a nuclear holocaust. What impact will the fear of AIDS have on the future behavior of men and women as they realize that a health crisis of historic proportions is at hand?

Because of AIDS, the sexually free lifestyles of the 1960s and '70s will never be safe again. In fact, many contend that the fear of AIDS has created a sexual counterrevolution. Evidence indicates that many men and women are changing the way they conduct themselves in sexual matters.

The death toll from AIDS will continue to mount for the next ten years and on into the next century. Will the effect of AIDS be so great as to disrupt the social order of this nation, as some now predict? This chapter provides provocative arguments that look beyond the immediate health crisis to consider some of the ways AIDS will affect society.

"To be blunt about it, . . . every sexual contact not made reduces the grim exponential probabilities that underlie the spread of [AIDS]."

AIDS Will Modify Sexual Behavior

Mickey Kaus and MacDonald Harris

Mickey Kaus is a senior writer for *Newsweek*. In Part I of the following viewpoint, he argues that the liberal sexual ethics of the 1960s have created the potential for a medical catastrophe. He claims that medical evidence now clearly shows the seriousness of AIDS, and in order to show its spread, there must be an end to promiscuity. Novelist MacDonald Harris, the author of Part II, contends that those attitudes of the '60s were an illusion. Sex was never meant to be free. Now, the price to pay for forgetting this lesson is sickness and death.

As you read, consider the following questions:

1. What are some of the reasons Kaus provides that justify panic among heterosexuals? What actions does he believe are necessary to control the spread of AIDS?
2. What, according to Kaus, was the problem with the sexual revolution?
3. What does Harris mean when he states that "there is no progress in sex"?

Mickey Kaus, "Needed: Some Healthy Panic Over AIDS," *St. Paul Pioneer Press and Dispatch*, January 20, 1987. Reprinted with the author's permission.
MacDonald Harris, "The Serpent Raises Its Head Again, And We Re-Learn a Lesson in Sex," *Los Angeles Times*, December 29, 1986. Reprinted with permission.

I

An editorial appeared in the *New York Times* Nov. 7 [1986] headlined "Don't Panic, Yet, Over AIDS." It dispensed this advice: "The likelihood of transmission in a single sexual encounter seems small. . . . The smartest thing to do now is to resist exaggerated fears of heterosexual transmission—and to fund more drug treatment programs."

One can almost see the editors congratulating each other on their level-headedness, on avoiding the sensationalism of lower-class journals and anti-AIDS fringe groups like the Larouchies. But as a result of such level-headedness, thousands, perhaps millions of Americans may die.

No Doubts About It

I am not a doctor. I leave to scientists judgments about the potential spread of AIDS in the "general population." Their judgments are in, and virtually none now doubts that AIDS spreads quite efficiently through ordinary heterosexual intercourse.

Estimates of the percentage of those infected with the virus who will come down with the disease—once vaguely comforting—have been steadily rising. The official estimate used to be 10 percent. Now it is 25 to 50 percent. But with an incubation period of up to 10 years, these figures are just guesses. Doctors at the University of Frankfurt in West Germany recently concluded that 75 percent of those with the virus will develop AIDS within seven years. Between 1.5 million and 3 million Americans already have the virus, estimates Dr. Robert Redfield of the Walter Reed Army Medical Center. That includes one out of every 14 to 18 people in New York City, according to the director of AIDS research for the city's department of health, Dr. Rand Stoneburner.

Dr. Halfdan Mahler, head of the World Health Organization and one of the major "don't-panic" spokesmen of months past, recently admitted he had been wrong. "I thought, 'Wait and see. . . . I definitely admit to a gross underestimate.'"

Two Approaches

But you don't need to be a doctor to reach some judgment as to what to do about the AIDS threat. Laypersons can at least make a crude estimate of the costs and benefits of various approaches—in particular the responsible don't-panic approach versus what might be called the hysteria approach.

I am not talking here about the hysterical fear of non-sexual, casual transmission. There the reassuring evidence is strong, although the human costs of hysteria are fairly high—AIDS kids kept from school, AIDS victims denied employment and ostracized. This sort of hysteria should be fought.

I am talking about hysterical, possibly exaggerated fears of sexual transmission. That, scientists tell us, is the way AIDS is contracted. But how paranoid should our society be in its sexual habits?

Under the don't-panic approach, promiscuity decreases but does not vanish. People exercise more care with their sexual partners and put their faith in condoms. Some, especially people who do not read the *Times* or believe the government, may not even take these precautions. This seems to be the current status quo.

I have a well-educated, well-informed friend who has decided she has nothing to worry about as long as she does not have anal sex with strangers. That still leaves plenty of possibilities. Others are even more resistant to hysteria and resolute in their lifestyles, believing the doctors have cried wolf once too often.

On the other hand, we have the prospect of panic. Whipped into a fever of fear, people virtually stop having non-monogamous sex. Ancient prohibitions on adultery are revived. Kissing is avoided (unless absolutely necessary). "Loose women" and philandering men are considered dirty. Crash programs (perhaps, as the *Times* warned, "overzealous" ones) spend millions of government dollars spreading fear of AIDS. Prostitutes are driven underground. AIDS blood-testing becomes widespread, and more and more potential carriers are notified.

Tom Gibb. Reprinted with permission of Heritage Features Syndicate, Washington, DC.

Each of these approaches might prove mistaken. But given the long incubation period, we would not know until it was too late. What are the down-side costs of error for each approach? Here they are:

• If the calm, responsible approach proves insufficient, millions die.

• If the hysterical approach proves unnecessary, the cost is . . . well, what? A great many Americans will lead impoverished or non-existent sex lives. Others will have their blood checked for AIDS even though they would rather not know. Still others whose behavior we have heretofore not found shocking will be stigmatized by a revived puritan morality.

These costs are not trivial—until you compare them to the potential costs of the don't-panic approach. To be blunt about it, what is more important, casual sex or avoiding a medical holocaust? Even if the AIDS catastrophe proves less sweeping than feared, every sexual contact not made reduces the grim exponential probabilities that underlie the spread of this (and other) diseases.

The Sexual Revolution

The logic supporting hysteria is pretty obvious. It is also pretty obvious that something, aside from sober responsibility, is preventing editorial-writers and policy-makers from reaching this obvious conclusion. On the right, the belief that homosexual sin is to blame for AIDS encourages ideologues to overlook the inconvenient truth that good old heterosexual sin is now just as deadly.

But for most of us the problem is the opposite: defensiveness over the seeming demise of the sexual liberation of the 1960s in both its heterosexual and homosexual aspects.

The realization of sexual tolerance on a mass scale was a major cultural achievement that, like cheap gas, we would not miss until it disappeared. Along with most of my post-World-War-II generation, I both subscribed to this liberated ethic and attempted to take advantage of it. For homosexuals, of course, the revolution was even more dramatic, as was the subsequent promiscuity.

Medical Case Against Promiscuity

Today, none of us wants to admit that we made a mistake, that this wonderful experiment was an epic social blunder, even as it becomes painfully clear that the venerable, inane prejudices against free sex had an ulterior hygienic function.

But recognizing the overwhelming medical case against promiscuity does not require a return all the way to bundling boards and the closet. Nor does it necessarily mean that the world of promiscuity we built and enjoyed was, somehow, immoral. But we have to confront the possibility that much of our agreeable modern lifestyle is unsupportable, even if it is not wrong in any moral sense. Certainly it will be unsafe to ever again allow gay bathhouse levels of promiscuity—it is just too efficient a method of spreading disease. (After AIDS, it will be some other disease).

Perhaps once the AIDS crisis has passed it will be possible to rebuild a modestly promiscuous culture of the sort clearly preferred by responsible editorial writers. I certainly hope so. But for now, the responsible course is irresponsible. The course of prudence is to panic.

II

The '60s were an exhilarating time, the time when all grew up. Some of us were called Flower Children then, and there was a childlike quality about the way we all lived. Everything we did was OK. You could wear your hair funny and dress any way you wanted, you could make love with anybody, any time, because you now had The Pill, and you could have a lot of fun with "psychedelic" drugs because they just bent your mind a little—they didn't break it. And there were no more taboos about words; you could say them all out loud, even the four-letter ones.

We had been liberated totally, and permanently. Or so we thought.

Prudence Could Save Thousands

For the millions of Americans currently infected or dying from AIDS, both breakthroughs and warnings to change their behavior will come tragically late. But prudence could save thousands of people in the U.S. who have yet to be exposed to the virus. Their fate will depend less on science than on the ability of large numbers of human beings to change their behavior in the face of growing danger.

Kathleen McAuliffe, *U.S. News & World Report*, January 12, 1987.

Then a few years ago we heard for the first time about another four-letter word, and it was an ugly one. It was a bad business, no question about that, but for a while it didn't bother us very much. It only affected Haitians, gays, drug users—people familiar to us only from the pages of L.A. Weekly and National Geographic. We weren't going to say it's their own fault or God's punishment; still, if they had been a little more like us. . . . It can't happen to us, we thought—we who live in the suburbs, have white skins, brush our teeth and believe that we are heterosexuals.

We know now that that smug immunity was an illusion. Heterosexuals *can* get it, and even "innocent" children through blood transfusions. It's spreading at an alarming rate, and there's no cure in sight.

We're scared. After all the sophisticated contraceptives we've seen come onto the market, each one better than the one before, we've come back to that old joke of our high-school years, the condom. (We used to say it was "like taking a shower with your socks on.") We're not reassured by the doctors telling us that we'll be OK if we don't do certain things. What if they're wrong? And what if I make a mistake?

In matters of love it's getting dark all around us. In the Middle Ages lepers were denounced from the pulpit and driven from human company, forced to wear bells to warn others of their presence—a crude analog of the quarantining and compulsory testing now called for in some quarters. Some doctors and nurses have refused to treat gays. Will we be the next ones they refuse to treat, we who have always made love missionary-style?

The fear of sex is coming back, the fear we had when we were very young, the fear of pregnancy, the fear of disease. And it seems that drugs aren't all that hot an idea, either. We see newspaper headlines that might have been written by A.E. Housman back in the darkest of Victorian times: "On an athlete dying young." Next the Ultimate Censor will appear and tell us not to use dirty words.

A Forgotten Lesson

When I was a child we were all terrified of polio. Everyone knew somebody who had gotten it; even the President of the United States was not spared. In those pre-Salk days there was no cure for it. Now we're back where we were then. And it's not just a matter of staying out of swimming pools in the summer; you can get a fatal and incurable disease for what you do in the privacy of your bedroom.

Sin has been reinvented, and we are reminded of something we had forgotten—that the wages of sin is death. Taking our showers with our socks on, we know once again the sour and ludicrous compromises of our youth.

What's going on anyhow? Have the '60s been repealed? Can we do whatever we want or not? We have gained, or regained, knowledge—that knowledge of good and evil that is the fruit of Eden. We know now that no matter how often the Fat Broad in the cartoon strip B.C. hits the snake with a club it will creep back into the funny papers. We know now . . . that there is no pill you can take, nothing you can shoot into yourself, that will make you happy, not without making you a lot unhappier in the long run. We know now that dirty words are not very eloquent; they're boring and disgusting, as our mothers told us. We know now that love is never free, that everything has a price.

Maybe they will find a cure for AIDS, but the '60s are over and they're not coming back. We suspect now that this shadow that hung over us when we were young, and hangs over us again, was *meant* to hang over us. The fear of night, the fear of death, is permanent. It is something we have to live with. It does not mean that happiness has been abolished, and it doesn't mean that you have to stop being gay, however you take the word. We can still love one another, but now you have to do it with caution, and with one eye to the doctors to be sure the way we're doing it is all right. We're back where we were, and it serves us right.

Sexual Habits Must Change

In the U.S., acquired immune deficiency syndrome is spreading—slowly, imperceptibly and inexorably. The calming of fears by public-health and government officials, as well as journalistic restraint, have been admirable in preventing panic, particularly regarding the risks of casual contact. However, it is extremely difficult to modulate public concern while simultaneously making it clear that many people—heterosexuals as well as homosexuals, physical-fitness fanatics as well as intravenous drug users—will have to voluntarily change their sexual habits. While there is energetic and ingenious research in progress with promising results, it cannot be assumed that a cure or vaccine will emerge within the next several years. For practical purposes, at this time the disease must be considered uniformly fatal.

While avoiding alarmism, one must realize the profound consequences of erroneous judgment in this matter. Most carriers of the virus bear no distinguishing marks. While those who have overt signs of illness are not easily mistaken, it is the behavior of the apparently well that is responsible for most of the current transmission. New relationships are constantly being formed and consummated; but the semi-carefree days of easy intimacy are gone. Caution in sexual matters is now a matter of necessity.

J.D. Robinson, *The Wall Street Journal*, January 22, 1987.

The '60s were an illusion. In the heady atmosphere of those days we believed that we had emancipated ourselves from the Human Condition, in which everything that men do is necessarily imperfect. Now we're back with the Existentialists we read in the '50s; we're responsible for everything we do, for every flea we kill. Looking at those doomed people in the news, we know that we will always be human and that there is no real progress—not in the arts, certainly not in politics, perhaps not in medicine, and above all, a thing we should have realized, there is no progress in sex. Milton had it right in the 17th century; he hailed Wedded Love but he hated that Serpent, the one that has now raised its head again.

"Only rarely does one find people so worried that they have changed their behavior."

AIDS Will Not Be Enough To Modify Sexual Behavior

Katie Leishman

Katie Leishman is a writer and editor who lives in New York City. She first reported on AIDS for *The Atlantic Monthly* magazine in 1985. The following viewpoint is excerpted from a later report in which she investigates changes in life-styles. She concludes that despite a growing risk of infection, heterosexuals are reluctant to modify their sexual behavior.

As you read, consider the following questions:

1. Why, in Leishman's opinion, do people perceive themselves to be immune to AIDS?
2. Leishman describes one man as being an encyclopedia of AIDS. What did this man mean by his statement that his fear of AIDS was intellectual?
3. Leishman concludes that safe sex is in the mind of the beholder. What does she mean?

Katie Leishman, "Heterosexuals and AIDS," *The Atlantic Monthly*, February 1987. Reprinted with the author's permission.

[In 1986] Dr. Thomas Peterman, of the Centers for Disease Control, in Atlanta, oversaw a study concerning transmission of HIV (human immunodeficiency virus), the principal AIDS virus, in families of persons with transfusion-associated infection. It was one of the first studies to assess the relative rates of sexual transmission from men to women and women to men. Not surprisingly, among people who did not have sex with infected partners there was no transmission. Among the sexually active couples, of the fifty men who were infected, eight transmitted the virus to their wives; of the twenty women, one transmitted the virus to her husband. It is of interest that the partners who became infected had all had only vaginal intercourse and reported fewer encounters after the transfusion than partners who did not become infected. One spouse became infected after only one exposure, another after eight. Obviously, the study documented that the disease was transmissible from men to women and women to men, but the varying rate of transmission provoked many questions. Do some men and women transmit the virus more efficiently? Or are some people more susceptible? Might someone have sex with a partner hundreds of times without transmission occurring, whereas the first time the infected person slept with someone else, transmission would occur?

The Question of Risk

The most important question, however, is one with which the study was not concerned, and it is a behavioral one, involving those couples who knew that one partner was infected. Why were any of these people—understanding that one could transmit a lethal virus to the other—willing to have sex without a condom? There have since been other American studies of transmission rates between infected people, such as intravenous drug users and hemophiliacs, and their partners, which incidentally document a strange phenomenon: many people who know they are at extraordinarily high risk nevertheless dispense with even minimal precautions. Confronted with such data, health officials must blanch at the prospects for influencing the behavior of the millions of people who don't believe themselves to be at any risk of exposure at all. . . .

One cannot speak about transmission rates in the general public until a large pool of infected individuals has formed at one remove from the primary risk groups. That pool is forming now. Even if heterosexually transmitted cases continue to be a secondary feature of the epidemic in the United States, the crucial questions that men and women outside of monogamous relationships—and many people in them—must ask themselves are, Am I at any risk of exposure to the virus? and more frightening, since ten years can pass before someone exhibits any visible sign of infection,

Have I ever been exposed? Whether the risk is one in ten or one in ten thousand, the risk is there. . . .

Each month yields new revelations from the behavioral research related to AIDS, much of it coming out of San Francisco and almost all of it concerned with gays. Public-health officials around the country must assess that data, keeping certain questions in mind. How do people behave when they know they are infected or at risk? What is the value of AIDS education programs?. . . Finally, to what extent can the behavior and attitudes of homosexuals be related to those of heterosexuals? . . . Much about the epidemic already suggests that ironclad distinctions between gays and straights serve no one and may cost some people their lives. . . .

Heterosexuals Still Trivializing AIDS

Many heterosexuals are still trivializing the implications of the presence of the AIDS virus in our midst. The Government is being laudably cautious in mounting this campaign, they believe, but where are the figures which will back up theories for the heterosexual transmission of the virus? There are only a handful of reported heterosexual cases in Western Europe that can be directly attributable just to straight, missionary position bonking, they seem to be reasoning, and while they will admit to the logic of the eventual spread of the virus to their environs and contemporaries, there really doesn't seem to be any impelling reason not to do it without a condom to this sweet young thing at their side. Maybe in six months or a year there might be some urgency but not now, not tonight, not between me and her/him.

Tim Clark, *Time Out*, January 21/28, 1987.

AIDS as it relates to heterosexuals presents an additional problem for behavioral-modification theorists: the risk cannot be defined. In general, the higher the degree of risk that can be projected for a particular individual, the easier it is to affect his behavior. The perception of a high risk and a catastrophic outcome combined might be expected to induce the greatest motivation to change, while a low risk and a negligible outcome should have little impact. When the perceived risk involved is as low as it is for most heterosexuals thinking about AIDS, the perceived severity of the outcome may not matter. According to [Dr. Lawrence] Green [the director of the Health Science Center at the University of Texas at Houston], people can take probability into account "as long as it is in their own betting experience—anything per ten or hundred." He adds, "But once you are into the thousands, it doesn't make much difference if it is one in one thousand or one in ten thousand. Most people can't relate to it, and it is easy for denial to take over. For those people who do perceive a risk at those levels, it will be a go or no-go decision to change.". . .

There are people who worry with seemingly little to worry about and people who don't worry who seemingly ought to. Only rarely does one find people so worried that they have changed their behavior. And these people—in particular, uninfected heterosexuals who have stopped having casual sex because of AIDS—very often deprecate themselves, describing themselves as hypochondriacal, irrational, paranoid, or neurotic. There is no question that AIDS provides a good excuse for men and women who were afraid to enter relationships anyway. And people who worry obsessively about germs now feel vindicated. But the number of people making real changes seems slight, even in places where information about AIDS is readily available.

AIDS Impact on Behavior

[In 1986] the San Francisco AIDS Foundation conducted a telephone survey of 400 randomly selected heterosexuals, 60 percent men and 40 percent women, one third minority, two thirds white. The subjects were asked to evaluate, on a scale of one to ten, how much impact AIDS had had on their sexual behavior. The mean response was four. Thirty-three percent said that AIDS had had no impact; 35 percent gave responses from two to five. Two thirds of respondents, then, rated the impact at five or below. Respondents were asked what types of people they believed to be at risk for getting AIDS. In San Francisco, with the largest per capita rate of AIDS in the country at the time, only seven percent of those surveyed said that sexual partners of people in risk groups were at risk.

Respondents were asked whether they had considered taking the antibody test, which has received enormous publicity in San Francisco. Five percent had taken the test and 31 percent didn't know it existed. Of those who knew of the test but hadn't taken it, 22 percent said they might, and 77 percent thought it was unlikely that they would.

The first statistic is perhaps the most interesting. A growing number of sexually active heterosexuals, especially in cities with a substantial caseload of AIDS patients, are considering taking the test. Most states have test sites, partly subsidized by the federal government, where the test is administered at no cost and sometimes anonymously. (Health clinics usually charge between $80 and $100, and at a private physician's office the fee can be as high as $300.) Perhaps straight men and women are willing to take the test because they do not have the strong reasons to fear that they are positive that many gays do, and because they are less concerned about confidentiality and civil-rights discrimination than are gays. In the New York City metropolitan area, where by the most conservative estimates of the health commissioner 500,000 people are infected, it is not unusual to find in one office several people who have considered taking the test and one person who already has taken it.

An AIDS Encyclopedia

In one such office, a law firm in Newark, a thirty-two-year-old attorney was working one afternoon when a friend, a partner in the firm who is known to sleep with many women, came in and sat down, white as a sheet. "Did you hear National Public Radio last night?" he asked. "The World Health Organization has written off—completely written *off*—four central African countries because the level of AIDS infection is so high."

Not Everyone Is Scared

One New York psychiatrist who treats young, sexually active patients says she sees a bell-shaped curve of fear. "There's a spectrum of reactions from blithe indifference to almost phobic anxiety, and most people fall in the middle. They have normal anxiety," says Dr. Zyra DeFries, assistant professor of psychiatry at Columbia-Presbyterian Medical Center. . . .

But not everyone is scared. If Dr. DeFries is right about a bell-shaped curve of anxiety, then many people have not modified their behavior. Ellen Krauss, 24, feels safe traveling in an insular, private-school, Upper East Side crowd.

"We're all preppies, even though we don't describe ourselves that way, so we think that this AIDS thing is not affecting us at all," she says. "We think it doesn't affect our class." Her sense of security would be shattered, she says, if she discovered that someone in her set had the disease. . . .

Samuel Learner, a 29-year-old investor, considers AIDS more a topic of cocktail conversation than a real threat. He concedes that he doesn't know much about AIDS. For instance, Samuel thinks he's got as good a chance of getting the disease from some imagined homosexual waiter who spits in the food as from sex with a stranger. He has cut out affairs with the "fringe element" of women who have many lovers, but Samuel continues to see a number of women.

Lucy Schulte, *New York*, March 3, 1986.

"Don't tell me about Africa," she said. "What are *you* doing?" Like many well-educated professionals who are sexually active, the man had become an AIDS encyclopedia without changing his habits. He knew the public-health budgets of several nations around Lake Victoria, the seropositivity rate among newborns there, and the results of every study of hepatitis among gay men in New York during the early 1980s. He had started to worry about

AIDS a year before and had become really worried after a discussion with some old friends several months earlier.

"I don't usually discuss sex with other men," he said later, "but somehow we got to talking about how many women we'd slept with in the past ten years. I went first and said, 'Oh, about three hundred,' thinking that was perfectly normal. I was appalled when the other men spoke up and the closest anyone else came to that number was about thirty. I didn't know I was an aberration.

"This advice 'Know your partner' is just ridiculous. The idea that, given the incubation period for the virus, you might have to think back seven or eight years—that terrifies me. I don't know the people I slept with then. In fact, I didn't know them when I was sleeping with them. I started doing some geometric progressions and figured out that I'd been exposed to tens of thousands of people.

Intellectualized Fear

"My fear is intellectual, though. It doesn't translate into my daily life. I have talked about AIDS with my current partner, whom I've seen for about two years. I have thought how wonderful it would be to know for sure you were antibody-negative and then be strictly monogamous with someone else who was and who you could trust to be faithful. I guess they used to call that marriage. In essence she and I do have a kind of pact. ["In essence" meant, it turned out, that he averaged one sexual encounter a week outside the relationship, often with one of the women he already knew.] She and I discussed the possibility of our both taking the test, and rejected it for the obvious reason: one of us might not be negative, which would immediately end the relationship right there.

"For me, knowing the results of the test would only be good if it told me I was negative. I am very frightened of the social aspect of the disease. The curtailment of sex would be the least of my concerns. I am more moved by affection than by sex. What I couldn't stand to lose would be the sense of connection, other people's good opinion of me. I'm afraid if I found out I was positive, I wouldn't want to go on living. I just can't take rejection. In this case ignorance is bliss, although you can't allow ignorance to create a danger for someone else. So I know what I have to do: use condoms. Have I done it? No." (For all that he knew about AIDS, he did not know that a person could be infectious and have no visible symptoms, or that condoms were recommended for oral as well as vaginal sex.)

His colleague in the office planned to take the antibody test. When she called her doctor's office for an appointment, the nurse said disgustedly, "You don't have AIDS. Don't worry about it." For two years the woman had dated a man who, she believes, was bisexual. Now she is planning to donate blood in order to ascertain her antibody status—an option many people hesitate to pursue, because it takes much longer to learn results and cases of seropositivity are often reportable to state departments of health.

These two attorneys often work with a fifty-four-year-old insurance-claims investigator. He has already taken the antibody test. He got married in 1973, but in 1985 he and his wife separated for eight months, during which time he had a girl friend and occasionally engaged in swinger group sex, which he had practiced regularly throughout the sixties and early seventies. The man tested negative. "If I had tested positive, I wouldn't have known how to conduct myself around my children," he says. "There is so much the doctors don't know about contagion. These swingers, they're mostly professionals, and they think the scene is safe. They're just kidding themselves."

Frighteningly Sluggish Response

The AIDS epidemic has entered the worry stream, the 4-o'clock-in-the-morning concerns. If we do not worry for ourselves, it's for our friends, family, children.

Nevertheless, it is remarkable how little actual behavior has changed. . . .

Many continue to focus on sexual morality instead of the deadly amorality of a virus. We have not yet made a crucial shift in our priorities, putting health first.

Ellen Goodman, *St. Paul Pioneer Press Dispatch*, January 27, 1987.

The magazines in which swingers advertise their charms and through which they make contact with each other are now full of assurances that the people in the photographs are "squeaky clean." The presidents of several swinger clubs around the country insist that swingers are more conscious of hygiene and disease than the average crowd at any singles bar, and that they are pre-screened in a way that isn't possible at, for example, a disco. "Everyone who calls me asks about AIDS," says the president of a 400-member club in Chicago. "I tell them I'm not a doctor. I can't screen people physically, but I can psychologically. I ask someone who wants to apply about their family background. I check out the way they dress, their educational level, their profession, and the rest.

"No one has taken the blood test in the group," he says. "There has been no discussion of using condoms. Definitely, there has been a greater tendency toward oral sex lately, and anal sex was eliminated without anyone having to mention a word. I would say about twenty percent of the men are bisexual and seventy-five percent of the women. I noticed that people have been avoiding the bisexual men recently. Everyone is questioning their swing partners more carefully, but no one is overly concerned. In five years we have had no major health problems." Such claims notwithstanding, reported outbreaks of sexually transmitted diseases in swing clubs in Minnesota recently led to a CDC study. One hundred and thirty-four members (seventy-five men and fifty-nine women) of swing clubs in the Twin Cities volunteered to be tested for HIV. None of the men but two of the women were positive.

Many single men and women across the country describe a kind of radar that they think they have for safe or clean partners. The word *picky* comes up a lot. These people say that they know just what questions to ask at a first encounter. Quite often the accounts they give of their own amorous histories do not jibe with reports from close friends and ex-lovers, especially concerning the number of partners the people reporting have had, which they underestimate. William Darrow, a research sociologist at the CDC, says, "If I've learned one thing in twenty-five years of this work, it is that people's anecdotal accounts of their sexual experiences aren't worth much.". . .

Safe Sex?

Strange days—and nights—lie ahead. It is true that there are still only about 1,100 cases of heterosexually transmitted AIDS. But it is also true that there were fewer than a hundred three years ago. The same numbers can be used to make a case for worrying or not worrying. Whatever happens, people will never get enough of tales of the epidemic, any more than they will tales of American slavery or of Nazis and their captives; the subject is subliminally pornographic, at once appalling and erotic. There is a certain excitement in having a legitimate reason—even a responsibility—to discuss in public what nice people have never discussed.

As the incidence of AIDS continues to rise, so will panic. But if fears, federal funds, and education alone are sufficient to alter people's most private habits, it will be for the first time ever. The changes that people at risk have been willing to make have not been sufficient. The impact of television could make a critical difference, especially if health officials and advertisers coordinate their efforts. Much is being asked of condoms, with all their frailties. It could be months but will probably be years before transmission of the virus is fully understood. Until then, safe sex is in the mind of the beholder. It can't hurt to think of the virus as having an intelligence, and a commitment to survival that exceeds that of many people.

197

"Because of AIDS, America may begin to look a lot like it did in the 1950s."

AIDS Will Transform Society's Morals

Cheryl Russell

Cheryl Russell is editor in chief of *American Demographics*, a monthly journal that defines statistical characteristics of the population for business purposes. In the following viewpoint, Russell states that statistics show that people have a greater fear of dying from AIDS than of the many other more likely causes of death. She concludes that this fear of AIDS will cause significant changes in family behavior patterns.

As you read, consider the following questions:

1. What statistics does Russell use to support her belief that compared to other causes of death, the numbers of AIDS deaths are trivial?
2. What are the changes in family behavior patterns that Russell predicts are likely to happen because of society's fear of AIDS?
3. What ingredient does Russell state will be missing between husbands and wives in the future? What will be there instead?

Cheryl Russell, "Fear of AIDS May Re-Create the Virtuous '50s," *The Wall Street Journal*, March 30, 1987. Reprinted with the author's permission.

AIDS will kill 14,000 Americans this year, according to projections by the Centers for Disease Control. Car accidents will kill three times that number.

Americans are more afraid of AIDS than they are of the many things more likely to kill them. Among the two million Americans who will die this year, AIDS will kill less than 1%.

More Important Causes of Death

In contrast, heart disease will kill nearly 800,000 Americans, and cancer will kill almost 500,000. Pneumonia, suicide and cirrhosis of the liver are far more important causes of death than AIDS. In numbers of deaths, AIDS ranks with emphysema, kidney failure and murder.

But AIDS has come a long way. Just four years ago, AIDS killed only one-tenth as many Americans as it will this year. Back then, it ranked with tuberculosis as a cause of death.

According to projections by the Centers for Disease Control, AIDS will kill 54,000 people in 1991. Even so, AIDS fatalities will account for less than 3% of all deaths. The Centers will not project AIDS cases or deaths beyond 1991 because no one knows how many people have been exposed to the virus, how the disease will progress or whether a cure will be found.

The impact of AIDS is most dramatic for one demographic segment of the population—men aged 20 to 49—and in two geographic areas—New York and San Francisco. For the nation as a whole, however, AIDS is an insignificant disease in absolute numbers of deaths.

A Blip in Morality Statistics

AIDS has been likened to the plagues that struck Europe in the Middle Ages. Like the plague, AIDS is fatal, but, unlike the plague, it is much harder to catch. The Black Death that struck Europe between 1346 and 1350 killed one-fourth of the population in 1348 alone, mortally wounding feudal society. AIDS would have to kill 60 million Americans in a single year to have the same demographic impact. By 1991, AIDS will have killed about 180,000 Americans during its 10-year existence in the U.S. During those 10 years, more than 20 million Americans will have died—AIDS will be no more than a blip in our mortality statistics.

While the numbers are trivial, the fear is not. The fear of AIDS— not the disease—will transform our society if a cure is not found soon. A disease that strikes the sex act with the deadly force of AIDS—half of AIDS victims die within 12 months; all eventually die—hits at the core of human society, because sex creates the family. Though AIDS deaths will not amount to much between now and 1991, the fear of AIDS will change the demographic structure of our population as it changes our lives. Unlike the plague, adults can control their exposure to AIDS. As people change their sexual behavior to avoid the disease, they will change the American family.

Fear of AIDS and Sex

The fear of AIDS will end the sexual revolution. After a 25-year hiatus, once again there is good reason to say no: Fear of death is a cold shower for casual sex, a more effective deterrent than fear of pregnancy. This fact is likely to make marriage more popular, especially among the young. Today, 59% of women aged 20 to 24 have never married, up from 28% in 1960. For men aged 20 to 24, 76% are single today, up from 53% a few decades ago.

Young people might marry earlier if they decide that one-night stands are not worth dying for. As AIDS deaths increase, more young people will know an uncle, a brother or a friend who has died of AIDS. Knowing one person who dies of AIDS will do more to change the behavior of young adults than a year's worth of lectures by the Surgeon General or Phyllis Schlafly.

The fear of AIDS will bring sex education to the public schools and make condom ads commonplace. With fewer unmarried people in the population and less sexual experimentation among them,

Steve Kelley, reprinted with permission.

the number of teen pregnancies and abortions should fall. Today, 81% of all abortions are to unmarried women, and 61% are to women aged 15 to 24. As the abortion numbers drop, the heated debate over abortion is likely to cool.

The fear of contagion may do what the fear of God cannot—bind husband and wife together till death do them part. AIDS is likely to make divorce a last resort for unhappy couples. Since the mid-1970s more than a million couples have divorced each year. Given current divorce rates, one-half of the marriages of today's young adults will end in divorce. AIDS may significantly reduce these odds. Why let go of a safe sexual partner when it's so dangerous to find another? Marriage counseling is likely to boom as couples struggle to stay together.

There are 45 million more households in the U.S. today than in 1950, but only 17 million more married couples. Married couples were 78% of households in 1950; now they are only 58%. As the fear of AIDS forces people to cling together, American suburbs and cities could become increasingly populated by the married, many of whom will regard the unmarried with suspicion and alarm. The married will be the clean, the unmarried the unclean, especially if states require AIDS tests for couples planning to marry.

AIDS may even spur another baby boom. As people marry earlier and stay married longer, family size could increase because women will be at risk of becoming pregnant for many more years than they are today. Married women who find themselves unexpectedly pregnant are less likely to have an abortion than single women. The result could be more babies and larger families. Because most young couples cannot afford the luxury of a stay-at-home mother, however, they will need day-care services to help them raise their children.

The Glue That Binds

Because of AIDS, America may begin to look a lot like it did in the 1950s. Virginity will be in, early marriage popular, divorce frowned upon, babies everywhere and family life back in vogue. One ingredient will be missing from this happy scene, however: The glue binding many husbands and wives together will not be love and faith in each other, but fear and distrust of everyone else.

"The burden of maintaining social cohesion—if society is to cohere in the face of chaos—will shift to the elderly."

AIDS Will Transform the Social Structure

Abigail McCarthy

Abigail McCarthy is a columnist for *Commonweal*, a liberal Catholic magazine. In the following viewpoint, she states that society will face serious consequences if a cure or vaccine for AIDS is not found. McCarthy argues that the death toll from AIDS will be greatest among those between the ages of 19 and 40, people in the prime of life who are responsible for maintaining social order. The loss of the middle generation, she contends, will shift the responsibility of caring for society to the elderly.

As you read, consider the following questions:

1. How does McCarthy support her belief that deaths from AIDS will mean a population disaster for society?
2. What does McCarthy state are the burdens of society that the elderly will have to assume?
3. How might society benefit from the loss of the middle generation, according to McCarthy?

Abigail McCarthy, "The Elders Among Us, AIDS: A Demographic Challenge," *Commonweal*, March 1987. Reprinted with permission.

It seems to be human nature to take perverse delight in predictions of disaster. We regale each other with details, with this or that statistic, fortifying our gloomy forebodings. We listen with fascination each evening to broadcasters forecasting doom in sepulchral tones and leaf hastily through the morning papers for further documentation. This seems especially true of our reactions to predictions of demographic disaster.

Predictions of Disasters

Just now the demographic news centers on AIDS. And it is grim indeed. The highest health officer in the land, Secretary of Health and Human Services Otis Bowen, has said in no uncertain terms that if we can't find a vaccine or a cure, "we face the dreadful prospect of a worldwide death toll in the tens of millions a decade from now." The spread of the disease to heterosexuals has been clearly documented; it is expected to account for almost 6 percent of the cases in the next few years. More than one million Americans are thought to be infected today—and are infecting others. Words like "plague" and "scourge" are appearing in the headlines. It is almost too much to take in. We teeter between panic and denial.

We have yet to concentrate on one of the most serious consequences of the projected death toll: *The people dying are, and will be, for the most part, young adults and persons in the prime of life.* They are those to whom any society looks for creativity and productivity. In this country, some industries—the entertainment industry for one—are already beginning to feel the effect of loss. *Time* magazine tells us that in central Africa, where AIDS is rampant in the general population, governments are just beginning to face the meaning of deaths of so many between the ages of nineteen and forty. These are their "best and brightest," those in whose educations their governments have invested heavily. Their loss could mean, at the least, a serious slowing in African development or, at worst, the destabilization of their nations.

Shouldering the Burden of Society

In the Western world, where those in the middle years are already straining between double burdens and caring for and educating the young and providing a life with dignity for the old, what will this pending population change mean? Surely one thing it will mean is that the burden of maintaining social cohesion—if society is to cohere in the face of chaos—will shift to the elderly.

Even before AIDS was seen as a significant factor, demographers were calling attention to the aging of our populations. Twelve percent of Americans are over sixty-five; in Europe the number is over 15 percent. Retirement states like Florida see the numbers of those aged eighty-five and over tripling by the year 2000.

203

Statistics like these have been cited as cause for alarm because of the accompanying decline in the birth rate. The focus has been on the cost for society in pensions and social security, plus the ever-increasing need for health care. "What you're going to see in the years to come will be staggering," says Martin Coyne, Florida's president of the Federation for Aging Research. Premier Jacques Chirac of France has been quoted as saying, "in demographic terms Europe is vanishing . . . our countries will be empty. No matter what our technological strength, we will be incapable of putting it to use."

Society Is Facing a Demographic Disaster

Every American will eventually pay a price for the AIDS epidemic. The price will include increased taxes, increased insurance rates, and some degree of lost freedom. The population most affected by AIDS is at the peak of their earning power. Without their energy, productivity, and consumption, the economy will be crippled, resulting in declining business conditions and an eroding tax base. In addition, there will be an eventual loss of leadership, managerial, and creative talent certainly equivalent to that lost in a major war. Our nation must respond effectively, coherently, and immediately.

We believe that if our nation continues to react to the AIDS epidemic in convulsive lurches we are doomed to an extraordinarily grim future.

James I. Slaff and John K. Brubaker, *The AIDS Epidemic*, 1985.

But now perhaps, in the face of the new and worsening threat, we need to examine the elderly population in terms of its strengths instead of its weaknesses, as potential contributors to society rather than only as consumers of its benefits. There is a pale parallel to the coming crisis in the period after World War II in Europe—and to some extent in America as well. The middle generation had been cut off in its youth. The great war losses delayed the handing on of leadership. (There were the women, of course, but that is another story.) It was the period of old men in charge—of Churchill and Truman and Eisenhower, of de Gaulle, Adenauer, and the others.

The Young Elderly

Already it has been recognized, although not emphasized, that the majority of the elderly are active, self-sustaining and in good health.

They are seen as "the young elderly"—those aged sixty-five to eighty as contrasted to "the frail elderly"—those over eighty. Their business is sought after as their percentage of the buying and investing population becomes more apparent. They are a political force as any politician who threatens Social Security or Medicare knows. Their organizations have multiplied.

The resources of these elderly are also already being drawn on by society. The great troops of volunteers once provided by middle-class women (now largely in the work force) are being replenished by the retired. The service industries are recruiting the elderly as part-time, even full-time workers, because they are found to be more industrious, more efficient, and less given to absenteeism than the younger workers available. Reports are that the younger workers at their side learn from, and are inspired by, the older ones.

The Call to the Elderly

It is possible that the growth in the older population is providential. It is time for the old among us to lift their sights and to see to what they are called. If, as panic grows and the ugly results of fear manifest themselves, the elderly gather and summon their political and organizational skill, their generosity, and their wisdom to address the problem, we may get through a bad patch of world history with much that is good to be handed on to the still untouched young.

"There is much . . . that gay men must give up."

AIDS Will Transform the Homosexual Lifestyle

Seymour Kleinberg

In the following viewpoint, Seymour Kleinberg argues that the behavior that homosexuals have used to identify themselves as individuals and as a culture since the gay liberation movement of the 1970s has become physically dangerous. He calls upon fellow gay men to be more introspective in determining what it means to be gay. Kleinberg is the author of *Alienated Affections: Being Gay in America,* and a teacher at the Brooklyn Center of Long Island University, Brooklyn, NY.

As you read, consider the following questions:

1. According to Kleinberg, what deeper meaning did promiscuity have for gay men in the 1970s?
2. Why does Kleinberg think that even if a cure for AIDS was found tomorrow, the gay lifestyle of the 1970s would not return?
3. What attitude toward society does the author think gay men should give up because of AIDS? What change would he like to see in society's view of gay men?

Seymour Kleinberg, "Life After Death," *The New Republic,* August 11 & 18, 1986. Reprinted by permission of THE NEW REPUBLIC, © 1986, The New Republic, Inc.

The effort to assess the meaning of one's sexuality—anyone's sexuality—has rarely been characterized by clear thinking or frank self-examination. Arguments and accusations about moral responsibility certainly don't help matters. Such confrontations are, rather, an invitation to defiance, rationalization, and rhetoric. Yet the time for such an assessment is upon gays, literally as a matter of life and death.

Gay Men Are Changing

Some gay men have been changing, in both unexpected and predictable ways. Former activists are now middle-aged and more prosperous than ever before in their lives. They have steady partners and more settled domestic lives. Even the majority who are single have found that the age-ism of gay culture has altered their sexual lives as much as AIDS has. Surprisingly, I find those for whom the caloric value of every mouthful of food was instantly tabulated, who were tanned all year round at the playgrounds of the Caribbean or Long Island, who never missed a day at the gym—they are the men who are putting on weight, and spending time on fund-raising, or working at the Gay Men's Health Clinic or elsewhere. One does not have to be political, or even to read with any regularity, to be civic-minded.

Some have refused to change; they search for safe places to practice old pleasures. Latin America and the Caribbean have long accommodated homosexual men with their informal bordellos, their "muchachos" who are partners to passive men but who do not think of themselves as homosexual. It is only a question of time before these gay men spread AIDS to other islands near Haiti, from which they probably first brought it to the mainland. It is hard to gauge the state of mind of such men. They may be filled with rage and seeking revenge. They may fatalistically believe that their behavior doesn't matter. They don't feel they are doing anything wrong, or they don't care. They have no moral sense, or they are immoral. It's bad enough to live in dread of dying an awful premature death. Yet to be filled with desire for revenge, or to be without desires at all, even for ordinary dignity, is a terrible way to live or die. I assume that such men act less from conscious indecency than from pure evasion. To emphasize sexual desire and desirability is a very effective way to mask anxiety. The habit of promiscuity doesn't allow much room for introspection.

Sex as a Liberator

Promiscuity is a broad term. For some men, it means serial affairs or brief erotic relationships. For others, there are no relationships at all; sexual encounters begin and end with momentary arousal. And for some men, promiscuity is all of these—having a lover, and having someone else, and having anyone else. Pro-

207

miscuity is time consuming and repetitious. Still, it also has another history and meaning for gay men; and it is that history, and that meaning, with which gay men in the shadow of AIDS must grapple.

A Forced Reexamination

"During the seventies, the gay movement here created an almost totalitarian society in the name of promoting sexual freedom. It evolved without any conscious decision, but there was so much peer pressure to conform that it allowed no self-criticism or self-examination. At some point, there would have to be less sexual, political, and visual conformity. People grow up and change. But AIDS forced a reëxamination in a way that few issues do. What we're seeing now is a revolution. We're seeing a reëvaluation of life and relationships and what being gay is all about. We haven't got the answers yet, but at least the questions have been posed."

Sam Puckett, quoted by Frances FitzGerald, *New Yorker*, August 28, 1986.

In the last 15 years or so, until AIDS appeared, promiscuity had been a rich if not invaluable experience for gay men, uniting a sense of liberation with a politics of resentment, a feeling of living at the modern edge with an outlet for aggressions created by long-held grievances. Such a combination is explosive, of course, and anti-intellectual. But gay men did not invent sexual liberation. They merely stamped it with their hallmark of aggressive display. Casual sex, freed from commercialism, seemed a glamorous portent of a society free from sexism. After "Stonewall," the riot at a New York bar in which gay men successfully resisted police arrest and inadvertently inaugurated gay liberation, gay activists felt they were going to redefine the old terms, junk the guilt and the remorse. They were already discarding with contempt the shrinks and the moralists, paying some of them back for the years of misery they had helped to create, the self-dislike they had urged gays to internalize for the sake of what now seemed merely propriety. Out the window went "sick" and "bad." Many could hardly believe they were jettisoning that dismal baggage.

Gays Became Visible

Those years of sexual opportunism were a time of indifference to psychological inquiry. Description was a higher priority. After so much silence, the need to explain, and the desire to shock, were first on the agenda of gay writers and intellectuals, while the majority of gay men were exploring an exhilarating sense of relief in discos, bars with back rooms, and the baths. The politics of that eroticism had as much to do with ego as with eros: gay men said that sexuality did not diminish social status, to say nothing of intellectual or professional stature—no matter how vividly it was practiced.

In the early '70s, when movement politics was at the zenith of its popularity, the values it promoted were very seductive. It said the old romantic pieties were a slavish imitation of straight society, where they were already undergoing vigorous scrutiny from feminists. If women and blacks could use politics to demand that society acknowledge they had been unjustly treated, why not gay men? . . . But for the most part, neither the victories nor the defeats changed the daily lives of gay men and women very much. With or without sodomy laws, most lived without concern for legality. It was understood that the principal struggle was psychological, a demand first for recognition, then for acceptance; the bold terms in which that demand was couched guaranteed the right to pursue a sexual lifestyle of their own choosing. After Stonewall, gays chose to be very visible. . . .

Sex as Politics

The more that sex dominated the style of life, from discos to parades, with rights secured or not, the less need most men felt they had for politics—and the less others, such as lesbians, feminists, and minorities, felt the gay movement offered them. For gay men sexual politics became something oddly literal. Both before and after the movement, promiscuity was honored as the sign of an individual's aggressiveness (no matter how passive he was in bed). . . . But most homosexuals want to be conventional. They are no more imaginative, courageous, or innovative than their neighbors. They want a good life on the easiest terms they can get. Many regard as uninteresting the activism that a handful of men and women are devoted to.

By the late '70s, movement politics displaced flamboyant effeminacy. . . . The dominant image of rebellion was no longer the defiant queens with their merciless ironies but powerful, strong bodies modeled on working-class youth. This new image exposed the erotic ideal of gay male life more clearly and responsively than anything since classical Greece. It was a vast improvement. Liberation freed gays from a lot of burdens, and one of the biggest was to end the search for masculinity among the enemy.

But paralleling the rise of the macho body has been the decline of the health of the male community—a nasty coincidence, if you believe in coincidence. The deeper truth, however, is that the very values that motivated us to look strong rather than be strong are the same values that elevated promiscuity as the foundation of a social identity. AIDS is mobilizing many to work in agencies caring for the ill, allowing them opportunities for sympathy and generosity—but that, too, is not the basis of an identity. What is killing you is not likely to give you a sense of self.

Even if AIDS were cured tomorrow, the style and identity of gay life in the '70s and '80s will be as dated as the sexual mores of closeted homosexual life are now. Many men may rush back to the baths, but it can no longer be the liberating experience it was. AIDS has nullified promiscuity as politically or even psychologically useful. AIDS has replaced one set of meanings with another. It has now become mythic as the dark side of sexuality. Thanatos to Eros. The life force that is the sexual drive has always had its counterpart, and AIDS is the most dramatic juxtaposition of the need for another and the fear of the other, of pain and pleasure, of life and death, in modern medical history. From the ancient Greeks on down, without a moment's interruption, the lesson has been the same: unfettered sexuality means death, whether through dishonor, the wrath of the gods, or nature itself. We are the heirs of those legends. AIDS, like a blotter, has absorbed those old meanings.

An Adolescent Coming of Age

AIDS seems to have affected gay men in two contradictory ways, making some more likely to come out and incorporate their homosexuality more centrally into their lives, while others have become less willing to associate with the gay world, more guilty and denying of their homosexuality. Thus it is difficult to say with much certainty just how the epidemic has affected gay life, despite the frequent comments that it has led gay men to go beyond a preoccupation with sex and partying to a new evaluation of community and family. "This disease marks the end of gay life as we know it," said one person with AIDS in Los Angeles. . . . Sometimes the gay community is compared to an adolescent now coming into middle age and taking on responsibility for others and for future generations.

Dennis Altman, *AIDS in the Mind of America*, 1986.

There is much, then, that gay men must give up. The loss of sexual life, nearly as much as grief and fear, compounds deprivations, and no amount of civic work or marching to banners of Gay Pride compensates for it. The most dramatic changes have occurred among those large numbers of men who have become abstinent, assuming a sense of responsibility to themselves if not to others. Not only must gay men refrain from what alone gave them a powerful enough identity to make a mark on the consciousness of society, a behavior that replaced society's contempt with the much more respectable fear and anger, but they must cease to think of themselves as unloved children. And they must do both

210

before they have evidence that society accepts them or that their own behavior has meaning for each other more nurturing than it has been. It is very hard to give up a sense of deprivation when little that created it has disappeared, and worse, when one is beset with fear.

No Group Responsibility

One thing, however, is clear: gay men are not acting in concert. If gay men sensed they belonged to a recognized community, instead of struggling still to assert their legitimacy, the task would be simpler. If they felt the larger society was no longer so adamantly adversarial, they could give up the sense of injustice that makes talk of social responsibility seem hypocritical. And if their own experience with each other had provided them with bonds deeper than momentary pleasure, they could trust themselves to act as a group in which members assumed responsibility for each other. . . .

Those men who act irresponsibly in the midst of this crisis betray their isolation, their failure to feel they belong either to a gay community or to a larger one. They perceive the demand for accountability as a demand from strangers. Society has not acted as the surrogate family in which we all develop our loyalties and moral sense. In fact, too often it acts just like the families of gay men: filled with contempt or indifference.

Gays Must Question Themselves

Many gays are now relieved that sex is no longer a banner issue. It is not even so important that we all stand up to be counted; enough of us have stood up to satisfy the curious. Instead, much as other groups in American society have done, the gay community has had to reassess more profoundly its relationship to the larger society. Customarily, that relationship has been adversarial. Now, for the first time in my memory, the gay community expects help. It hopes for sympathy from heterosexual society. It expects that those who are ordinarily silent will be uncomfortable with such neutrality when orthodox religious leaders proclaim AIDS the scourge of God upon homosexuals, or when politicians exploit and promote fear.

AIDS has made it necessary for gay men to begin questioning themselves. For too long we have lived as if we were driven, too impelled to know what we were doing and what, consequently, was happening to us. It takes perhaps half a lifetime before one is capable of the introspection (not self-absorption) necessary to make sense of the past and thus act as a morally free adult. The same is true of groups. There are moments in history when groups, too, must tell the truth about themselves.

Distinguishing Fact from Opinion

This activity is designed to help develop the basic critical thinking skill of distinguishing between fact and opinion. Consider the following statement as an example: "In the United States the number of reported domestic cases of heterosexually transmitted AIDS has increased by over 200 percent in the past year." This is a fact with which no one who has looked at the research could disagree. But consider another statement about AIDS: "The smartest thing to do now is to resist exaggerated fears of heterosexual transmission." This statement expresses an opinion on how to react to AIDS facts. Many people, especially those concerned about contracting AIDS, may disagree with it.

When investigating controversial issues it is important that one be able to distinguish between statements of fact and statements of opinion. It is also important to recognize that not all statements of fact are true. They may appear to be true, but some are based on inaccurate or false information. For this activity, however, we are concerned with understanding the difference between those statements which appear to be factual and those which appear to be based primarily on opinion.

Most of the following statements are taken from the viewpoints in this chapter. Consider each statement carefully. *Mark O for any statement you believe is an opinion or interpretation of facts. Mark F for any statement you believe is a fact.*

If you are doing this activity as a member of a class or group, compare your answers with those of other class or group members. Be able to defend your answers. You may discover that others will come to different conclusions than you. Listening to the reasons others present for their answers may give you valuable insights in distinguishing between fact and opinion.

If you are reading this book alone, ask others if they agree with your answers. You will find this interaction valuable.

> *O* = *opinion*
> *F* = *fact*

1. Ironclad distinctions between gays and straights serve no one and may cost some people their lives.

2. Doctors at the University of Frankfurt concluded that 75% of those with the virus will develop AIDS within seven years.

3. You don't need to be a doctor to reach some judgment as to what to do about the AIDS threat.

4. AIDS may provide the ultimate test of strategies for modification of sexual behavior.

5. Most states have AIDS test sites, partly subsidized by the federal government, where the test is administered at no cost and sometimes anonymously.

6. Straight men and women are willing to take the test because they do not have the strong reasons to fear that they are positive that many gays do.

7. In New York City, the health commissioner estimates that over 500,000 people are infected with AIDS.

8. Half of AIDS victims die within 12 months; all eventually die.

9. Married couples were 78% of all households in 1950; now they are only 58%.

10. One night stands are not worth dying for.

11. Knowing one person who dies of AIDS will do more to change the behavior of young adults than all the lectures by the Surgeon General.

12. *Time* magazine stated that in central Africa, AIDS is rampant in the general population.

13. It is time for the old among us to lift their sights and to see to what they are called.

14. From the ancient Greeks on down, the lesson has been the same: unfettered sexuality means death, whether through dishonor, the wrath of the gods, or nature itself.

15. Some gay men have been changing in both unexpected and predictable ways.

16. Gay men did not invent sexual liberation.

17. Now, for the first time, the gay community hopes for sympathy from the heterosexual society.

Periodical Bibliography

The following articles have been selected to supplement the diverse views expressed in this chapter.

David Baltimore	"Quarantining Will Help No One," interview, *U.S. News & World Report*, January 12, 1987.
Joseph Carey	"And Now, A Worldwide War Against AIDS," *U.S. News & World Report*, April 6, 1987.
Barbara Kantrowitz	"Fear of Sex," *Newsweek*, November 24, 1986.
Kirk Kidwell	"The Protected Plague," *The New American*, April 13, 1987.
Kathleen McAuliffe	"AIDS: At the Dawn of Fear," *U.S. News & World Report*, January 12, 1987.
The New Internationalist	"The Politics of AIDS," March 1987. Available from P.O. Box 255, Lewiston, NY 14092.
Carrie Rickey	"Kiss Me Deadly: Dating Safe in the Age of AIDS," *Mademoiselle*, June 1986.
Bryan Robinson, Patsy Skeen, and Lynda Walters	"The AIDS Epidemic Hits Home," *Psychology Today*, April 1987.
Michael S. Serrill	"In the Grip of the Scourge," *Time*, February 16, 1987.
Martha Smilgis	"The Big Chill: Fear of AIDS," *Time*, February 16, 1987.
Jeannine Stein	"AIDS Launches Sexual Counterrevolution," *Los Angeles Times*, April 3, 1987.
Lindsy Van Gelder	"AIDS," *Ms.*, April 1987.
Claudia Wallis	"You Haven't Heard Anything Yet," *Time*, February 16, 1987.
Alfred Yankauer	"The Persistence of Public Health Problems: SF, STD, and AIDS," *American Journal of Public Health*, May 1986. Available from University of Massachusetts Medical Center, Worcester, MA 01605.

Organizations To Contact

The editors have compiled the following list of organizations concerned with the issues debated in this book. All of them have publications available for interested readers. The descriptions are derived from materials provided by the organizations themselves.

American Civil Liberties Union (ACLU)
22 E. 40th St.
New York, NY 10016
(212) 944-9800

The ACLU champions the rights set forth in the Declaration of Independence and the Constitution. The Foundation of the ACLU is involved with test court cases, opposition to oppressive legislation, and public protests. It opposes any action, including testing and contact tracing, that might endanger the civil rights of AIDS carriers. The Union's publications include the monthly *Civil Liberties Alert*, the quarterly *Civil Liberties*, and various pamphlets, books, and position papers.

American Foundation for AIDS Research (AFAR)
40 W. 57th St.
New York, NY 10019
(212) 333-3118

The Foundation was established to raise funds to support research on AIDS. The group is developing educational programs to prevent the spread of the disease. It maintains a speakers' bureau and also publishes pamphlets on AIDS.

American Red Cross AIDS Education Office
1730 D St. NW
Washington, DC 20006
(202) 639-3223

The organization operates a variety of community health education services and blood related services. AIDS education pamphlets, brochures, and posters are available from local Red Cross chapters. Many chapters offer video tape services, conduct presentations, and operate speakers' bureaus.

Catholic Charities of the Archdiocese of San Francisco AIDS/ARC Program
50 Oak St.
San Francisco, CA 94102
(415) 864-7400

The AIDS/ARC program was established in 1985. It offers an emergency health fund to help victims of AIDS/ARC with medical expenses. It operates a residential program for the homeless that includes behavioral counseling. It provides ministerial services to AIDS victims, their families, and friends. The organization publishes a newsletter and offers a pastoral packet that includes a list of pastoral resources.

Centers for Disease Control
1600 Clifton Road NE
Atlanta, GA 30333
(404) 329-3311

The CDC was established in 1973 as an operating agency within the Public Health Service. They are charged with protecting the public health of the nation by providing leadership in the prevention and control of diseases and by responding to public health emergencies. The Centers publish the pamphlets *What Everyone Should Know About AIDS* and *Information/Education Plan: To Prevent and Control AIDS in the United States*, and *The Surgeon General's Report on AIDS*.

Children's Hospice International (CHI)
1101 King St., Suite 131
Alexandria, VA 22314
(703) 684-0330

The organization's objective is to provide hospice care for children. It also encourages inclusion of children in existing and developing hospices and home care programs. CHI provides information to other hospices and is developing a program for the pediatric care of AIDS victims. It publishes a monthly newsletter and various brochures.

Eagle Forum
PO Box 618
Alton, IL 62002
(618) 462-5415

Eagle Forum is dedicated to preserving traditional family values. It opposes all anti-family, anti-morality, and anti-life programs. The Forum's views, based on biblical interpretations, include the belief that homosexuality is morally wrong. It publishes the *Phyllis Schlafly Report* which frequently includes statements on AIDS issues.

Family Research Institute
PO Box 6725
Lincoln, NE 68506
(409) 489-5324

The Institute believes that homosexuality is a major public health threat and must be controlled. It favors stern measures on homosexual activity. It publishes a newsletter and a number of pamphlets, including *Homosexuality and the AIDS Threat to the Nation's Blood Supply*.

Gay Men's Health Crisis (GMHC)
Box 274
132 W. 24th St.
New York, NY 10011
(212) 807-7035

The GMHC was founded in 1982 as a social service agency for the clinical treatment of AIDS. It provides support and therapy groups for AIDS patients. The group publishes a monthly newsletter and a booklet called *Medical Answers About AIDS*.

The Hastings Center
360 Broadway
Hastings-on-Hudson, NY 10706
(914) 478-0500

Established in 1969, the Center is a non-profit and non-partisan research and educational organization devoted to ethical problems in biology, medicine, the social and behavioral sciences, and the professions. In addition, the Center conducts special projects on the issues created by the AIDS epidemic. It publishes *The Hastings Center Report* which regularly includes material on AIDS.

Institute of Medicine and the National Academy of Sciences
Office of Public Affairs
2102 Constitution Ave.
Washington, DC 20418
(202) 334-2000

The Institute was established to identify, study, and report on the nation's major problems in health sciences and health care. It advocates the establishment of a National Commission on AIDS to coordinate an intensive, integrated attack on the disease and its spread. Among its publications are the report *Confronting AIDS: Directions for Public Health, Health Care, and Research* and numerous other studies regarding AIDS.

National Coalition of Gay Sexually Transmitted Disease Services
PO Box 239
Milwaukee, WI 53201
(414) 277-7671

The Coalition is a network for organizations that treat and care for AIDS patients. It provides an opportunity for organizations to share research and ideas for fund-raising and patient education. It also maintains a liaison between AIDS organizations and drug companies, health organizations, publishers, and other organizations interested in AIDS. The Coalition's publications include a periodic newsletter and an annual publication on safe sex.

National Lesbian and Gay Health Foundation (NLGHF)
PO Box 65472
Washington, DC 20035
(202) 797-3708

The group's purpose is to develop and coordinate interdisciplinary health programs and activities for lesbian and gay health organizations. It publishes quarterly and annual directories, a biennial sourcebook on gay/lesbian health care, and a quarterly gay/lesbian health book.

National Resource and Consultation Center for AIDS and HIV Infection (NRCC)
110 Greene St., Room 406
New York, NY 10012
(212) 219-8180

The NRCC is the AIDS and HIV infection department of the National Hemophilia Foundation. The Center serves as a resource for local and regional health care professionals, self-help groups, individuals, families, and the general public. The NRCC seeks to combat irrational fears and prevent discrimination by providing the most updated information regarding HIV, AIDS, and hemophilia. The Center publishes several reports including *AIDS, HTLV-III, and Hemophilia: Your Questions Answered*, and *Hemophilia and Acquired Immune Deficiency Syndrome (AIDS): Intimacy and Sexual Behavior.*

Shanti Project (SP)
890 Hayes St.
San Francisco, CA 94117
(415) 558-9644

Shanti Project is a volunteer counseling service offering support for those who have been diagnosed as having AIDS. The Project provides support groups, peer counseling, hospice care, and long-term, low-cost housing. It publishes a monthly directory and monthly and quarterly newsletters.

US Public Health Service
Public Affairs Office
Hubert H. Humphrey Bldg.
Room 725-H
200 Independence Ave. SW
Washington, DC 20201
(202) 245-6867

The Public Health Service is a government agency that publishes several brochures and pamphlets including *AIDS, Sex, and You, Facts About AIDS and Drug Abuse,* and *AIDS and Your Job: Are There Risks?* It provides additional information upon request.

Women's AIDS Project
8235 Santa Monica Blvd., Suite 201
West Hollywood, CA 90046
(213) 650-1508

The Project is a non-profit organization which provides education and support for women with AIDS. The organization believes that women with the disease are often overlooked. It works to alleviate the fears and isolation of women with AIDS. The organization also provides lab testing and health services. The project publishes the pamphlet *Women Address AIDS.*

Bibliography of Books

The following books and pamphlets have been selected to supplement the diverse views expressed in this book.

Books

Dennis Altman — *AIDS in the Mind of America.* Garden City, NY: Anchor Press/Doubleday, 1986.

American Medical Association — *AIDS from the Beginning.* Chicago: AMA Publications, 1986.

Gene Antonio — *The AIDS Cover-Up?* San Francisco: Ignatius Press, 1986.

David Black — *The Plague Years.* New York: Simon and Schuster, 1986.

John Brubaker and James Staff — *The AIDS Epidemic: How You Can Protect Your Family—Why You Must.* New York: Warner Books, 1985.

William A. Check and Ann Guidici Fettner — *The Truth About AIDS.* New York: Holt, Rinehart and Winston, 1985.

Institute of Medicine and National Academy of Sciences — *Confronting AIDS.* Washington, DC: National Academy Press, 1986.

Institute of Medicine and National Academy of Sciences — *Mobilizing Against AIDS.* Cambridge, MA: Harvard University Press, 1986.

James McKeever — *The AIDS Plague.* Medford, OR: Omega Publications, 1986.

David Noebel, Wayne Lutton, and Paul Cameron — *AIDS: A Special Report.* Manitou Springs, CO: Summit Ministries, 1986.

Jon G. Nengesser — *Epidemic of Courage.* New York: St. Martin's Press, 1986.

Pamphlets

American Civil Liberties Union — *AIDS: Basic Documents.* New York: American Civil Liberties Union, 1987.

Alexandra Mark and Vernon H. Mark — *Supplement to Pied Pipers of Sex.* Brookline, MA: Sabin and Mark, P.C., 1987.

Index